The Trillion D
Stress Solut

Modern Stress Management: From Stress To Success

Silvia Hartmann

First Edition 2015

DragonRising Publishing
United Kingdom

Published By
DragonRising Publishing
United Kingdom
www.DragonRising.com

Printed and bound by CPI Group (UK) Ltd, Croydon, CR0 4YY

Table of Contents

Foreword

Welcome, dear reader, to The Trillion Dollar Stress Solution.

This is a very passionate book, a very personal book.

I have done my best to transmit information and seeds of thought that will transform the way you think about the world, the people within it, and most of all, yourself.

The title of this book, "The Trillion Dollar Stress Solution" is based on the "Trillion Dollar Stress Pandemic" which has enveloped the world today.

Never in the history of humanity have so many people been so stressed, and that is in spite of the fact that we are richer, better educated and better fed than ever.

What's happening?

What is going wrong?

Well, I know the answer to this, and I'd like to share it with you.

Not only with you, but through you, with many, many other people as well.

Once you know and understand, it is simplicity itself.

Once you know, understand, and then start to apply it, your world will change for the better.

That's a pretty big claim, I am aware of that.

I am perfectly happy to stand behind this claim which is 100% based on my personal experience, on my research and on the results this research has produced over the last 25 years.

This is a fascinating story; I feel privileged today to be the one who is telling you about this; just as you may well feel privileged to tell another, or many others, when it comes to your turn in passing on this information.

I am German born, so I shall wish you many an excellent "AHA!" moment as you go through the chapters of this book.

It's a beginning, to be sure, a new beginning.

And that is always - very, very exciting!

Welcome to The Trillion Dollar Stress Solution!

Silvia Hartmann
August 2015

Prologue

In 2012, I met a stressed man.

I was doing an art project with volunteers, and amongst the volunteers was a gentleman of around 50 years of age.

He was very well dressed, wore an expensive watch and arrived in a very expensive car.

He seemed to be on top of the world, with a young and beautiful third wife, owner of a company with many employees, manufacturing high end machinery for export, owned a yacht, a plane, a mansion overlooking the bay, all the good things.

And he was so stressed that I was fearful he would drop dead of a heart attack or a stroke any second now.

There was a moment when my heart went out to him.

Here was a person who most people would never, ever suspect was so close to the edge.

He could not tell anyone.

Everyone relied on him.

His wife, his employees, their wives and children, his aged parents ...

He had no way of dealing with his stress.

And it was this gentleman who opened my eyes to the "Trillion Dollar Problem."

It became very clear to me that he was not in a good state to be making decisions that affected all those who relied on him.

It became very clear to me that he was not just one man, but a living example of what is happening everywhere, who walked into my studio that day.

It was then that I started to turn my mind towards what I could do for him, and all the others like him from a whole new perspective.

Decent, good people, trying to do their best, working themselves literally to death to fulfil their responsibilities, fighting themselves all the time, losing their mind, losing their health, losing their joy of life - what a nightmare!

To the global economy, "The Trillion Dollar Stress Pandemic" is the huge elephant in the room that nobody knows how to deal with.

To one single individual, it is true catastrophe.

Stress causes a loss of life, a loss of joy and a loss of what they could have contributed if they weren't stressed out of their minds - that's a loss to all of us, at a cost that I can't even begin to calculate.

What was even worse was that I had the answer to the problem, and I had this in my possession since 1993.

I had this answer because of animal behaviour studies we were conducting back then; I had discovered the missing X-Factor in the mysterious stress equation that the old scientific models simply could not solve, or even begin to explain.

When I laid out my findings to my esteemed learned colleagues, they turned on me and threw me out.

In the final meeting, I shouted at the head of the research group, "You know I am right about this! What is wrong with you that you won't publicly admit it?"

And he shouted back, "If you think I'm going to re-write 40 years worth of materials, my entire life's work, you've got another thing coming!"

There we have it.

Let's just keep going with the same old.

We don't want to re-write our pamphlets, published articles, training programs, learned books, scientific studies. It's too much work. Burying the truth is so much simpler ...

I will admit, my young aspect was so deeply shocked by this, she let them get away with it. She walked away and turned her back on the mainstream.

When 20 years later that gentleman turned up for my art project, I knew I had to give it at least one more shot.

I know what causes stress. I also know how to alleviate it.

Let me explain ....

The Harmony Program

The original animal based research program from the late 1980s and early 90s revolved around the so called "rage syndrome." This is diagnosed when animals go berserk and attack, seemingly without provocation, and without prejudice. It didn't matter if the target of the attack was known, unknown, friend, foe - in a rage syndrome attack, all of that was of no consequence.

All manner of things were being investigated as the cause for this; one candidate after the other was investigated and discarded along the way. Chemicals in the environment, genetic predisposition, previous traumas, allergies, general management, additives in food - none of it seemed to make any difference.

I worked with all of this intensively for over five years.

If you don't know me yet, I'm German born and have what might be called an obsessive streak; for those five years, I did nothing else. I took no weekends off, no breaks, no holidays. 24-7 I did nothing else, talked of nothing else, dreamed of nothing else; I was absolutely determined to find the cause for rage syndrome in social mammals.

And in August of 1993, I found it.

I found the "invisible something."

We call it "energy" now, and that's not being unscientific. The term "energy" is simply a place holder until we can find a more appropriate word. In the meantime, "energy" allows us to move forward with our investigations, when without it, we would remain stuck in the old.

Here is what I found.

There is an invisible something that is being exchanged between social mammals, such as dogs, horses, elephants, monkeys, dolphins and human beings.

This invisible something is needed - seriously, structurally, absolutely, in the same way that a creature needs food and water or **it will die**.

When this invisible something is in short supply, social mammals start to get stressed, then very stressed, and when it doesn't get any better, they will literally "freak out" and throw a final tantrum - our mysterious rage syndrome in action.

This is most likely an "ultimate, final survival effort" - like a zebra would thrash around in the jaws of a lion, a last ditch effort where whatever is left is thrown into the system.

After that, which cannot be sustained for long, the creature crashes and burns.

It is so low on energy that it will faint, or may die of a stroke, or a heart attack. If it survives, it may be significantly damaged and show all the signs of "autism" - an inability to connect with others of its kind to obtain energy from them, or to engage in normal social energy exchanges with them.

Back then, the young scientist summed it up as follows: (my current aspect's comments are in *italics*)

Attention Seeking Behaviour progresses through the following stages as the need (*for obtaining energy*) becomes more and more acute and more excruciating to the individual who is experiencing the energetic shortfall in a visceral, whole body experience:

1. Awareness

Here, the creature (child, dog, cat, horse) first becomes aware that the shortfall exists and begins to look around for a likely "other" who may fulfil this need.

2. Approach

The creature will start approaching the other and give minor signs that it is in need of attention. In an animal, this would be moving closer and presenting themselves whilst looking directly at the other.

3. Escalation

If the other ignores (read "refuses to provide the attention energy") this subtle approach, creature A will now escalate its behaviours to "break on through" the barrier of ignoring – make sounds, push physically, engage in behaviours that have previously worked to "gain attention."

4. Extreme Escalation

If these higher level behaviours are also ignored, the need turns to a pain and will now drive consecutively more extreme behaviour in turn in a direct cause and effect relationship. If the need is high enough, the creature may even attack.

5. Catastrophic Collapse

If still no energy is forthcoming, the system collapses in on itself in a catastrophic implosion which causes severe damage; the stage beyond rage is autism, where the creature can no longer elicit the energy required nor process it when it is being offered because of the damage sustained by the receptors of the energy processing system during the catastrophe.

Depending on the severity of the neurological/energetic catastrophe and the **age** of the creature at which the catastrophe occurred (obviously the younger the creature, the greater the impact on the system overall), some individuals may never come back from the autism stage and remain there forever.

From "The Harmony Program," Silvia Hartmann, 1993

Back in those days, I described the act of "energy seeking" as "attention seeking behaviour" - that's how we thought of it then.

9

Over two decades later, and I explain it like this now.

1. People (and at least all social mammals) really do have an energy system, an "energy body."

2. This energy body has nutritional needs, it "needs to eat" - but it needs energy, not burgers and fries.

3. In social mammals (such as people!) a significant amount of energy is supposed to come from other members of their own species.

Here comes the important bit:

4. It is our **emotions** which tell us when we need to go energy seeking.

What Are Emotions?

If you ask a doctor or a psychologist, you won't get any answer that makes any kind of sense to normal human beings.

If you ask me, I will tell you this.

1. Yes, we really do have an energy body!

2. This energy body transmits "how it feels" through emotions.

3. Emotions are sensations in the body that have no physical origin - emotions are the 6th Sense.

• Emotions *are* the 6th Sense.

Emotions are the feedback devices that tell us how our energy body is functioning.

We can't see our own energy bodies, and we can't see the energy bodies of other people, but we can *sense* them.

Our 6th Sense is exactly that - the feedback sensations transmitted from the energy body to our physical body.

"Do you know those sensations when your stomach is churning, your head goes hot, your hands start shaking and your knees go weak?

"That's what other people call emotions!"

Silvia Hartmann
The Trillion Dollar Stress Solution

11

Emotions Are Not In Your Mind, They're In Your Body

Emotions come in a range of physical experiences which increase in severity, the greater the need for paying attention to these warning signals becomes.

1. **Intuition:** At the lowest level, we have the fine, fleeting sensations that are called "intuition" or "gut response" that warn you of danger or tell you someone's lying to you.
2. **Emotions:** The mid range sensations of heat, pressure, coldness, tightness, heaviness that are "emotions" such as anger, sadness, anxiety, etc.
3. **Psychosomatic Pain:** The top end of emotions are so physically painful, they can be no longer distinguished from actual physical pain, and those are called "psychosomatic pain" - the strongest form of negative emotion known to mankind.

The Emotion Range Scale:
All these are emotions, movements in the energy body that transmit to the physical body.

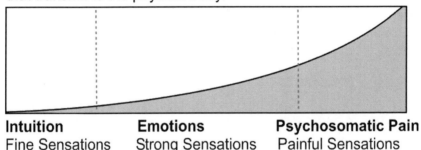

Intuition	Emotions	Psychosomatic Pain
Fine Sensations	Strong Sensations	Painful Sensations

All of these sensations are produced by the energy body and simply tell us what's going on.

Emotions are a feedback system like the flashing warning lights on the dashboard of a car. We have those warning lights because we can't "see" what the engine is doing, what's going on with the oil pressure or the water temperature when we're driving the car.

Somewhere, someone decided to disconnect these warning lights, especially in men who are supposed to "feel nothing at all, ever," thinking that this would cure the problem.

Fools ...

We will come back to this ...

In the meantime, the big news from The Harmony Program was that **low energy states in social mammals cause ("emotional") stress.**

Low Energy States Cause Stress

This stress gets consecutively worse, the lower the energy states become.

The creatures will show more and more antisocial, stupid, counter-productive, insane behaviours, the worse this becomes.

If it gets too bad, there is one last flare up of the super stressed system, our original rage syndrome, then it burns out and you are left with serious structural damage.

- **Energy body stress causes a direct, linear, predictable decline from sanity into insanity.**

Energy body stress and the behaviours it drives occurs exactly in the same way and the same order and sequence in little children, adults and old people from every race, cultural and societal background as it does in puppies, elephants, horses, sheep, monkeys, dolphins - this stress decline from sanity into insanity is structural, normal, natural and most of all, **completely predictable.**

This decline from order into chaos most likely goes further than that and represents a general law of nature, if applied to systems overall; but for our purposes here, it is enough to note that emotional stress is not something people have made up, or that it's "all in their minds."

Emotional stress is real, energy body stress is very real, and it has extraordinary effects on the behaviour, performance, state, social abilities and physical functioning of people.

**Emotions are not in your mind.
They're in your body.**

Silvia Hartmann
The Trillion Dollar Stress Solution

So Now, What Do We Do?

With having established to my personal satisfaction, and over a considerable period of time, with thousands of different creatures in many different scenarios, that I was right about the effects of energy body stress, it was time to ask the question, "So now, what do we do?"

We have a creature who is clearly stressed and misbehaving, *attention seeking* (read: energy seeking for survival!) in a big way.

We were taught that when a creature is naughty, we have to punish it.

We have to withdraw attention, or beat it up in some way, hurt it in some way, so "it learns its lesson."

Yet the Harmony Program authoritatively states that the problem is that the creature is low on energy in the first place.

How is making it even lower on energy going to make this a better creature?

The answer is, well of course, it isn't.

Beating up on a child because they were naughty doesn't produce "a better child."

It might produce a more silent child. A more scared child that is easier to control next time around. But it might also produce a child that grows up to be a very angry man who beats his wife and his children, is anti-social, can't control his temper, can't relate to other people properly, hates everyone, ends up in jail ...

The Harmony Program prescribes the theory of a different approach.

> *"If someone is hungry, feed them.*
> *"If someone is thirsty, give them something to drink.*
> *"If someone is low on energy, GIVE THEM ENERGY."*

In other words, reward the attention seeking behaviour with giving attention.

Reward energy seeking behaviour with giving energy.

Oh My God!

If the theory wasn't yet controversial enough, now we were in heresy country.

The entrainment to "punish bad behaviour" is so deep, so profound, so all encompassing, it was more than shocking to the research subjects of the young scientist who proposed nothing more than a few experiments with doing it the other way.

Reward bad behaviour?

"You'll create a monster!"

I don't know how many times I've stood with owners, parents, spouses, and said succinctly to them, "You have that monster on your hands already! Let's try a different approach, just to find out what would happen ..."

The few who were brave enough to try were completely amazed.

Among them was a husband whose wife "always annoyed him by talking at him when he was trying to read the paper in the morning."

He literally forced himself to drop the paper down on the first approach of his wife, just enough so he could make eye contact with her, and gave her the attention (*the energy exchange!*) she craved.

And instead of talking at him like a sledge hammer in rising tones and voices for the next half hour, the lady in question smiled, came over, gave him a kiss - and left him alone!

After 38 years of marriage, containing 365 days each where the same annoying story had been playing out, he was totally astonished by that.

I was astonished that this should astonish him so.

It wasn't a miracle. The poor woman needed a bit of attention. She got it. There was no reason to continue to annoy him after that.

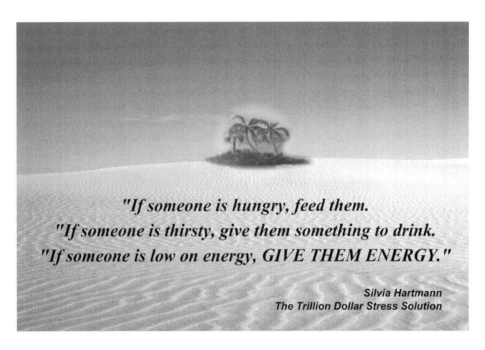

"If someone is hungry, feed them.
"If someone is thirsty, give them something to drink.
"If someone is low on energy, GIVE THEM ENERGY."

Silvia Hartmann
The Trillion Dollar Stress Solution

"If someone's hungry, give them some food ..."

That, however, was just the tip of the iceberg.

Giving attention, ENERGY, profoundly changed the behaviour (and the health!) of all sorts of creatures for the better. Of course, it made life so much happier and easier for those who had to deal with these creatures, like the man who no longer had his ears talked off first thing in the morning and finally got to read his paper in peace after 38 years of trying to ignore her.

15

To many people, the cessation of unwanted and annoying behaviours was as though a major miracle had happened, and they were ecstatic.

But that was not the end of the story - not by a long shot.

There was more to it than just that.

It wasn't that just the bad behaviours disappeared.

A whole new creature emerged from the Harmony Program.

A friendly, sociable, co-operative being that was far more intelligent, sensitive and capable than anyone had suspected before.

The wife didn't just leave her husband alone. She kissed him, smiled, and told him that she loved him!

That's not just "cessation of the bad behaviour."

It's the exact opposite - the inverse even.

We didn't go from bad to not bad any longer.

We went from bad to good.

We were moving into the undiscovered territory of positive emotions - and the true opposite of "stress" which isn't actually "no stress" but a totally different state of affairs we might as well call a whole new level of "success."

The White Space Of Happiness

Let us imagine a scale of all possible human emotions, let's say from -10 in the negative, via 0 Zero and then all the way up to +10, where the most powerful positive emotions reside.

At Zero, there is no more stress - but there is also, Zero success.

"No stress" is not the answer to anything at all. It's like having Zero money in your bank account, Zero friends, Zero food in the fridge.

It's not even a starting point, if you look at it like that.

Yet we all were so deep in the negatives, so terribly stressed, that the alleviation of pain to "absolutely nothing" was all we could hope for - just for the stress to go away, for the pain to stop, even just for a moment.

Zero is incredibly unattractive though - naturally. It's a very unfortunate place to be and you soon slide off again into the negatives, like trying to clamber up an icy hill and stopping midway to the top for a break.

There was "life beyond Zero."

We discovered a whole new, undocumented "white space of happiness."

An unexplored landscape of positive emotions, and what happens when we actively try to provide more energy.

The discovery of the effects of positive emotions proved to be one of the major building blocks of our Trillion Dollar Stress Solution.

When we were working with the Harmony Program in the mid 1990s, we discovered that the more you "fed" your target creature with positive energy, the more they started to change.

There was a tipping point when the bad behaviours would disappear - but if you kept on giving them positive attention beyond that tipping point, positive changes would come into being that were completely unexpected.

There was a little boy of five years of age who was wetting his bed every night. "Everything" had been tried, including old fashioned behaviourism, medication and electric shocks, and "nothing had worked."

The parents were so desperate, they tried that crazy new idea to reward the child with positive attention when he wet the bed. It took three nights, and the problem was gone.

They were so delighted, they continued with the positive attention ritual in the morning, which was simply going into the child's bedroom and greeting him with full eye contact, smiling at him unconditionally, giving him a hug and talking about something good, such as breakfast or a happy event in the day, something to look forward to.

The parents did this partially because they were afraid that the bed-wetting would start up again if they were to stop; and partially because it started the day

17

much better than it had before - with smiles instead of tears, as the father remarked.

What happened next?

"As if by magic" the previous fighting and jealousy between the boy and his younger sister stopped; he adopted a caring attitude towards her and was found teaching her to read one day.

The parents were completely astonished and talked of a miraculous transformations, couldn't believe their luck, were so happy at "getting a whole new boy and he's so wonderful!"

I was well used to these "miraculous, magical, unexpected side effects" that went far beyond simply solving the problem by then.

It made sense **if there are negative states, there have to be corresponding positive states.**

There was a whole world of interesting **positive emotions**, hugely powerful when it came to behaviour modification and healing all sorts of problems, easy to work with - yet nobody seemed to care about those at all!

Ending The Nightmare of Trauma

I became involved with people once I understood that what I had found with the animal behaviour was so structural, it extended to all social mammals, and started looking into human psychology, naturally.

What I found was as follows.

Psychology is a relatively new field which has strenuously tried to gain acceptance as being a "proper science."

In the absence of its own instruments, psychology has borrowed heavily from the existing medical model (the current scientific medical model of the Western World) and imported ideas, presuppositions and tools which are deeply unhelpful if you want to understand "what makes people tick."

The first problem comes from studying pathology - studying the diseased (liver, body, brain, mind) in order to learn about *disease*.

The study of disease and malfunction may have worked well for modern medicine, but when it comes to emotions, we are dealing with a different field altogether.

Endlessly studying crazy people is going to seriously skew the "knowledge base" of any field, as you can imagine. You end up with a mountain of data on what crazy people do, and no data on normal people, and even less data on people who perform better than normal.

The other problem is the very definition of "health."

Psychology inherited a measurement device from the medical world called the SUD Scale. It measures pain (or "Subjective Units of Distress" as they like to call it) from -10 to 0 Zero.

In medicine, when it doesn't hurt any longer, you're cured, you're done, and the doctor's job is over.

So, you have a pain in the ass. You go to the doctor. The doctor cures that and now, there's no pain any longer. You feel nothing. You go away, cured.

The doctor makes no attempt to make your backside start to feel good, then truly spectacular. And of course, you don't expect them to do that.

But that's *medicine*.

In any form of real emotional healing, **"feeling nothing" is not a goal**.

"Feeling NOTHING is not a goal.

"It's a prescription for misery and a wasteland life."

Silvia Hartmann
The Trillion Dollar Stress Solution

"Feeling nothing" is at the very best, a step stone.

It is understandable to want to not feel pain any longer, but the human energy system, which communicates through emotions, **is not healthy yet when we "feel nothing."**

- **Healthy for the energy body is to feel great.**

To feel strong, powerful, happy, joyous - ecstatic, even.

There is a whole other side to the stress scale - the positive wing, the unexplored territory on the other side of human performance.

Which brings me to "the nightmare of trauma."

When I use the phrase, "We must end the nightmare of trauma!" I refer to the fact that present psychology is lost, stuck, mired and sunk in a world view that orientates on and revolves around past trauma alone.

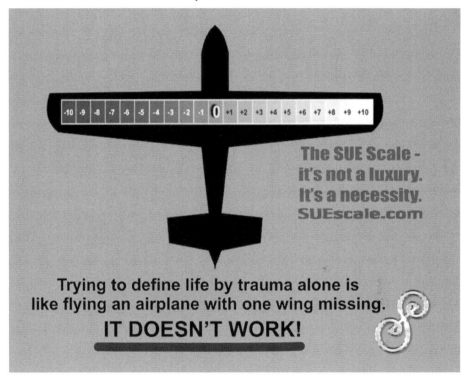

In order to help people in any shape or form, this focus on trauma exclusively is a labyrinth with no way out. If we want to understand people, if we want to actually help people lead better lives, we need to go beyond trauma, and in a big way.

It is true that trauma causes much suffering; even though there isn't a psychologist in the world today who can explain what actually happens in traumatic experiences to cause the problems they cause.

If you can handle the idea that people have energy bodies, and that these energy bodies can become injured in the course of life in much the same way as a physical body can become injured when they are shot in the stomach or in the head, then it makes perfect sense that stress and disturbed emotions should be the result.

But that's not the whole story.

People do not live their lives the way they do just because of trauma.

They are also guided by "Guiding Stars" - moments of high POSITIVE experiences on which they become stuck.

This happens to people who end up collecting warehouses full of Star Wars toys, have a shoe fetish, develop an internet addiction, always marry men who look like Uncle Bob, can't leave the house where their child was born, become the abuser after having been abused, eating themselves to death on strawberry ice cream ...

Guiding Stars are just as responsible for all manner of problems in people as are trauma events, yet current psychology doesn't seem to be at all interested in them. In fact, and as far as I know, my "Guiding Stars" paper from 2000 is still the only logical and comprehensive discussion of the effects of highly charged, positive experiences on a person, and on what needs to be done to get people unstuck so they can start to live again[1].

The reason there is no "body of knowledge" in existing psychology on Guiding Stars is because **the entire positive side of human performance is missing** - as a concept, as a reality, as a structural given and **as a goal**.

Now, we have the major pieces in place.

---

1   *For more information on trauma, Guiding Stars and how to deal with energy body events in general, please see "Events Psychology" by Silvia Hartmann, DragonRising Publishing 2009.*

The Story So Far ...

- People have an energy body.
- The energy body transmits information about its state of functioning via the 6th sense to the physical body.
- These sensations that have no physical origin are "emotions" (intuition, emotion, psychosomatic pain). This is our true 6th Sense.
- The energy body becomes stressed when it runs short on energy - its own fuel for life.
- The more stressed the energy body becomes, the more this affects the mind, and the body, causing malfunctions in thought, physical prowess, social abilities, and behaviour as well as the accompanying emotions with their physical sensations of pressure, pain, trembling etc.
- As everyone's energy body has been ignored from conception to death, almost all people on Earth today are suffering from major energy body stress, which is making them unhappy, over-emotional, sick and stupid. It is this which has caused "The Trillion Dollar Stress Pandemic."
- There is a whole other range of human functioning beyond the old Zero of Nothing, where positive emotions which come from a happy energy body reside.
- This "positive side" is virtually unknown, virtually unexplored and it is there where the solutions to our stress problems can be found.

Let's take a look at the bigger picture - meet the Energy Body Stress Chart.

23

The Energy Body Stress Chart

-10	So much stress damage that the system does not restore itself (catatonia)
- 9	Total stress, absolute system breakdown, complete mental, emotional and physical collapse - nothing is working any longer (epileptic fit)
- 8	Very high stress causes extremely severe disturbances (self mutilation, blind rage, "going berserk," "madness")
- 7	Very high stress causing extreme disturbances (extreme temper tantrums, self abuse, schizophrenic metaphors, "crazy ideas")
- 6	High stress causing high disturbances (temper tantrums, high end addictions, illogical thinking, immediate gratification, unstable, highly egocentric)
- 5	Full stress causing the symptoms normally associated with stress (irritability, inability to concentrate, not in control of thoughts and memories, communication failures, inability to enter rapport with another)
- 4	General stress (lapses in ability to control thoughts, emotions and behaviour, lack of long term planning ability, overexcited, overly (...), stubborn, closed mind, impaired communication skills)
- 3	Medium stress (talking, thinking and moving a too fast, trying to do too much, putting in more effort than the situation requires, lack of empathy)
- 2	Low Stress (slight impairment in emotional control, not entirely "clear" on future goals and current situations, impairment in social skills)
- 1	Very low stress (occasional flashes of uninvited thoughts and negative internal representations)
0	No stress (calm, tranquil, peaceful, no action required, resting, relaxing)

This is the negative side of the Energy Body Stress Chart.

It is *the only* side known to current psychology and current stress management. Everything stops at Zero, if you're going up, and it starts at Zero, when you're going down.

This is the pathology of psychology who borrowed the idea of "there is only pain, and no pain" from medicine, in action.

With Zero being the only goal, it all stops there, and we are living in a world where "the best a man can get" is ... NOTHING.

But nothing could be further from the truth. The truth is that there is a corresponding chart of positive energy body states. Here it is.

24

0	Energy flow at Zero (Zero emotions, Zero motivation, Zero inspiration)
+ 1	Very low energy flow (neutral, aware, occasional flashes of positive/interesting internal representations and emotions)
+ 2	Low energy flow (vague sense of potential, hope, feeling like "waking up from a sleep")
+ 3	Slightly improved energy flow (sense of wellness, feeling OK, smiling, beginning to move, noticing the present)
+ 4	Improving energy flow (breathing deeply, increased body awareness, more movement, feeling good, starting to think about the future, able and willing to communicate)
+ 5	Fair energy flow (feeling wide awake, happy, ready for action, wanting to take action, *wanting* to interact and communicate)
+ 6	Faster energy flow (feeling exciting physical sensations, more expansive thinking, feeling personally powerful, forward looking, enjoying communication, high social awareness)
+ 7	Very fast energy flow (re-thinking and re-organising concepts, expanded awareness, feeling powerful positive emotions, feeling alive, feeling love)
+ 8	High energy flow (picking up personal power, feeling delighted, making new decisions, very fast and very logical thinking, high social abilities of rapport and communication)
+ 9	Very high energy flow (delighted, unable to sit still, tingling all over, very excited, joyful, actively loving)
+ 10	Optimal energy flow (enlightenment experience, unconditional love, Zen state)

Take a moment to look at the complete stress chart, from -10 to +10.

Where are you right now?

Do you remember times when you were way up, and way down?

Where do you "normally" find yourself?

Think of other people you know. Does this make sense?

Think of animals you have known. Does this make sense?

Does what I have laid out here tally not with all the other books you've ever read, but **with your own personal life experiences?**

If yes, read on.

The SUE Scale

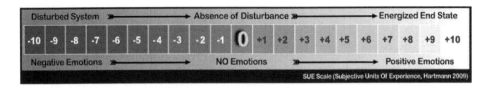

The SUE Scale (Subjective Units of Experience, Hartmann 2009) replaces the SUD Scale (Subjective Units of Distress, Volpe, 1969) to measure emotions, emotional disturbances, and in our case, emotional STRESS.

The fact that we would even have a "psychology instrument" that stops at Zero and doesn't acknowledge the existence of positive emotions is mind blowing in its own right - as is the fact that nobody seems to have challenged this, ever.

Clearly, whatever your emotional problems might be, to feel nothing at all is no sign of cure. At best, it is a step stone on the way to true emotional health, which we would find somewhere above +7.

Having no positive wing to a scale that measures human experience has many, many other horrendous repercussions. In hindsight, this is not surprising - playing with half a deck of cards is going to produce some very peculiar games.

In this circumstance, we are playing with a deck that has all the aces and all the trumps missing!

It produces a miserable game where no-one ever wins, no-one ever goes home happy, and the best you can hope for is to leave with Zero happiness at the end of the day.

This is the truly crazy world of current psychology; but it isn't for us here, because we are not talking about psychology.

We are talking about energy.

About the FACT that people really do have an energy body, whether science likes this or not; whether we have the mathematics capable of handling this or not, whether we ignore this or not.

Reality doesn't care about our delusions. It just punishes us for getting things wrong.

Reality gives us powerful feedback on what works, and what does not work.

So now, here we are. I've known all of this since 1993 but could not find anyone to listen to me, to take a look at this, because once you start talking about energy, everyone thinks you're crazy - right?

Wrong.

The people who can't sense energy are a tiny minority, if extremely vociferous and currently often placed in positions of high authority.

I had made some progress with explaining my findings among a small group of people who were ready for modern energism; but after my meeting with the poor stressed gentleman during the art project, I decided to find out what could be done so more people would get to know about this, and would have a chance to take control of their emotions, and thereby their lives, in a whole new and different way.

I decided that it was time for main streaming modern energy work -

- the physically felt, personal, experienced reality of our emotions;
- the huge, huge effects they have on everything we do;
- and what we had learned about how to change negative emotions to the positive side of the SUE Scale.

But how could I explain all of this to "the people"?

Did "the people" even want to know?

I had to find out ...

Main Streaming

So there I was, back at the art project with my poor stressed out business owner, wondering what I could do to help him, to help other people like him.

I realised that I could not learn about this by staying at home and talking to the same people I was always talking to - other energists, people who had already experienced and understood the benefits of working with energy.

Therefore, I took a whole year out of my busy schedule as the trainings coordinator and chair of The Guild of Energists, and went on a road trip.

Three road trips, to be precise.

One through England, Scotland and Wales.

One through Ireland and Northern Ireland.

And one through the United States of America.

I talked with real people I met along the way.

I talked with truck drivers, policemen, the ladies in a laundry. I talked with artists, writers, business owners, mechanics, entrepreneurs, retired folk, people from all walks of life.

One night, around 3am, I found myself in an all night coffee house near Dallas, Texas.

The night staff there was very low on energy.

There was an old man who had gone bankrupt because of medical bills for his wife. She was dead now and he lived in his truck.

There was a woman with heroin teeth, orange hair and many tattoos.

There was a young man who was very quiet and withdrawn.

They made me coffee and I told them that I was on the road because I wanted to learn about people. They told me about their lives, and I asked questions, about their hopes and dreams, their plans.

After 20 minutes, they were all smiling and talking. They had come to life. Around 4am, the quiet young man told me how much he had loved looking after the horses on his grandfather's farm, and how perhaps he should look for a job with animals ...

A bit of attention.

A direction of attention towards something you love.

There is more than just "no stress."

There is so much more than just "finding a bit of peace."

When energy rises, and our energy bodies come to life, everything changes.

Everyone transforms.

- ***People come together.***

People become far more powerful, far more loving.

I already knew we needed to get what I know about energy out there.

But it was right then, when I looked into that young man's eyes that I knew it had to be done NOW.

Fast.

Right NOW.

We all need to take charge of that Trillion Dollar Problem - it's **our problem**.

Everyone's individual problem, but all together, it is everyone's problem, everyone's business because stress transmits, and it affects us all in the end.

We are wasting not just our own lives living on the wrong side of the Stress Chart. We are wasting our best people, the best of all our people, and that is something we cannot afford to be doing any longer.

We need to raise not more money, but more energy.

You need energy to make that move from working the night shift in a coffee house to going out there and trying to find a job working with animals, a new job that will give you more energy, more joy, a step stone to a better life.

29

That's the same thing as a big company owner who has thousands of people to take care of needing energy to go out there and find new markets, new ways of surviving against the hard global competition in a recession.

It's the same thing again for a mother who wants to love her children but simply hasn't got enough energy left to give them the attention they need to grow up strong and healthy.

Stress is a serious, serious thing.

Energy body stress is a serious topic. It is a destroyer of lives.

Yet we can reverse it, and move out of those states - we can move from stress into success.

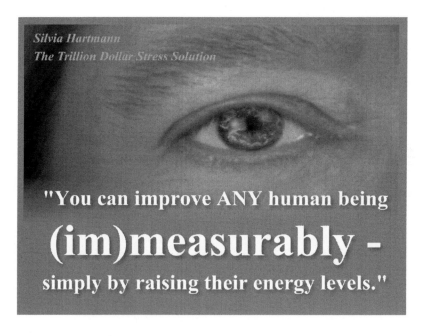

"You can improve ANY human being immeasurably -
simply by raising their energy levels."

Love & Logic

The Harmony Program and the Stress Chart, the SUE Scale with its positive wing that seems to be entirely unexplored to date, are all one model, and they all have one thing in common.

They are testable, predictable, reasonable and rational.

What I discovered is **extremely logical**.

A model that makes human emotions predictable and logical is something we've all needed for a very long time.

As always though, there are those undiscovered bonuses and benefits when we finally get things right.

Not only is the Harmony Program logical, it is also extremely loving.

The words of those prophets who talked of love as the greatest power in the Universe start to make sense.

I say this.

As both love and logic become purer, clearer, righter, they come closer and closer together, and eventually, you reach a place where love and logic are one and the same.

Not "different sides of a coin" - they are EXACTLY the same, **they are one**.

We can turn this around and say that as long as logic is loveless, it's not really proper logic yet, and as long as love remains illogical, it isn't proper love yet, either.

From this notion comes my favourite quote:

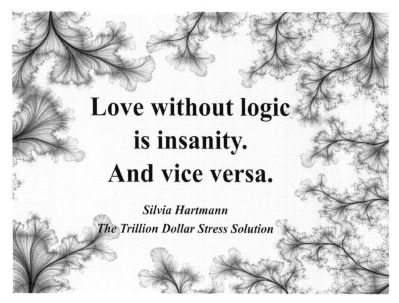

Love without logic
is insanity.
And vice versa.

Silvia Hartmann
The Trillion Dollar Stress Solution

When we are stressed, it seems that love and logic are not just light years apart, they are opposites of each other, at war with each other, in endless conflict with one another.

That's because when we are stressed, we become stupid.

The more stressed we are, the more stupid we become in a direct cause-and-effect relationship.

We become stupid, illogical, stubborn, judgemental, close minded, blinkered, short sighted - just as we become stressed, nervous, angry, afraid, paranoid, defensive, freaked out at the same time.

Add a little energy into those stressed systems, and matters change drastically.

On the right side of the Stress Chart, on the plus side, when we are in energy profit, we become smarter.

Much, much smarter.

We can calculate more complex systems, plan over time, hold the bigger picture, zoom easily into any details level and back out again.

We are in control of our minds and in control of our bodies.

This increase in intelligence, this leap into a higher order of thought and vision doesn't just happen for the chosen few who were born with the right genetics, into the right family, under the right stars in the sky.

This is so for absolutely everyone who is a normal human being.

A normal human being is someone who can manage to cross a street without being run over, at least on most days. This is so for you, and for me, and for him and for her over there as well.

That is so for industry leaders, beggars in the street, single mums on benefits, the aristocracy, the football player, the piano player, the pimp and the thief.

We become more intelligent - but **we also become more loving** as energy levels start to rise. I sum that up by saying,

**"The more you have,
the more you have to give."**

Below Zero, you are dangerously short on energy, and you will be "energy seeking" (attention seeking) from others. Dominance displays by a boss who is throwing himself around as though he had to compensate for a dick the size of a noodle is an example of that, as is endless whining, bitching and moaning by his harassed martyr secretary.

This is, of course, extremely annoying to others who likewise, have nothing left to give because they're stressed as well. In any team, family, company, that sort of thing goes from bad to worse if there's no-one there to stem the tide and turn the big waterwheel the other way.

Above Zero, you have as much to give as you have.

+1, you have very little and if you gave all of that, you'd end up in negative equity as well.

+5 and above, you're in a totally different place.

You can become charitable, compassionate, patient ... in other words, you can energetically afford to be generous with other people.

Kind.

Courteous.

Loving.

That has the side effect that you also become more popular.

People who "feel good to be around," people who "make you feel like a better person" when you are working with them, those people are highly attractive to others.

They earn respect, love and loyalty, and this further empowers them - the energy rich become ever richer.

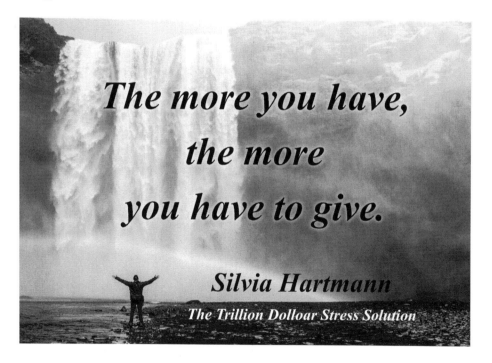

The more you have, the more you have to give.

Silvia Hartmann

The Trillion Dolloar Stress Solution

How many stressed people have sat in the darkness over the ages of humanity, sitting in darkness even as we speak, and with bitter envy and anger looked upon the "golden ones who live in the light and have all the love, all the luck, all the opportunity" - when they have less than nothing?

And wondered why?

And cried and came to the conclusion that there must be something horribly wrong with them as they dropped lower and lower on the energy scale, into crazy self mutilating territories and beyond?

I wish there was a way for me to reach them, and to say to them, loudly, with authority,

No! You're not crazy.

YOU ARE SIMPLY STRESSED.

No! You're not doomed!

You too can feel better, be shinier, attract more love and luck and everything good - you just need to (re)learn to raise your energy levels a bit.

And YES - this is so structural, it means <u>you too</u>.

It is so structural, it really means everyone.

It's nothing but the truth!

Logical People

The Harmony Program, expressed in the Energy Body Stress Chart and the SUE Scale, makes people logical.

It ends the idea that people are born bad, or just crazy as a species.

It ends the idea individuals may have that they're some kind of insane serial killer, and that is their true nature.

It also ends the idea that you're born a certain way, and there's bugger all you can do about it.

All of that is old.

All of that is based on crazy ideas, created by people who were clearly extremely stressed and couldn't think straight.

People are easy.

Treat them well, and they become better people.

Mistreat them, and they become worse people.

Duh.

What a revelation ...

And yet, this is scientific, religious and societal heresy.

The idea that you "make better people" by punishment and driving them into more and more stress, like lemmings of a cliff, is enshrined and taken for granted absolutely everywhere.

The most extraordinary example of this is a model at the very bottom of existing stress management dogma, and this blew my mind when I saw it for the first time.

The Great Lie Of "Beneficial Stress"

Subtitle: Yerkes-Dobson: Driving People Into Stress - Since 1908!

When I started thinking about creating a new Modern Stress Management program for the Guild of Energists GOE in 2015, I thought, well, let's have a look what is out there, what the "general consensus" is getting up to these days.

This is what I found.

This is a screenshot of the result of a 2015 image search on "stress management." You see the exact same model in variations over, and over, and over again - some form of upside down soup bowl.

If you haven't met this yet, let me introduce you to ...

"The Hebbian Stress Curve."

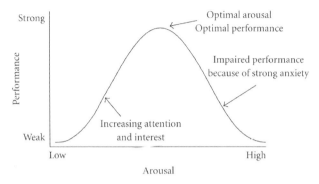

This is the model on which all of so called stress management at this time is based.

The "Hebbian Stress Curve" is a 1950s version of an older model, "The Yerkes Dobson Law of Arousal" from 1908 (yes, 1908!) and it basically proposes that you need to stress or hurt "just right" folk so you can get "optimum performance" out of them. Check this out:

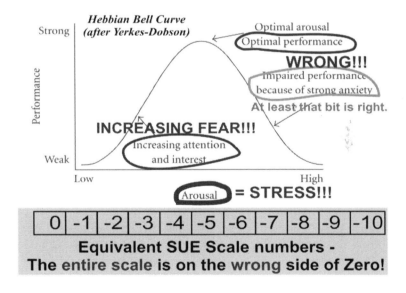

The great lie of "beneficial stress."

There is no such thing as beneficial stress.

All stress is bad, and if it isn't bad, then it probably wasn't stress, but a higher energy state such as excitement, from the positive side of the SUE scale.

37

I immediately knew that this model was totally wrong, and **DANGEROUS**.

Driving people into stress from a resting state is a recipe for disaster on every level.

How could it be that all these people were singing the wrong song from such a faulty hymn sheet?

I dug a little deeper and found that our 1908 friends Yerkes and Dobson were shocking sleeping rats with electricity at one end of a maze.

- If they didn't shock them enough, the rats just went back to sleep.
- If they shocked them quite a bit, the panicked rats ran as fast as they could through the maze to get away.
- If they shocked them too much, the rats would go absolutely berserk and totally fail at anything other than flailing around insanely (Rage syndrome!)

From this, our friends Yerkes and Dobson concluded that "optimum performance" occurs when you shock your rats just right. This research has been taken to mean that you need to "hurt your workers just right" to get "the best performance" out of them!

Ladies, gentlemen and all most wonderful readers, this is ridiculous on too many levels all at once.

First of all, human doings are not running blindly through a maze, or at least, they shouldn't be.

The worst thing with this study which became a "law" (!!!) that then everyone just repeated as though it was God's word handed down from the stars themselves, is that it totally misses the effects of POSITIVE AROUSAL.

The sleeping rats were shocked. That's it.

We never learned just how rats who woke up HAPPY would perform in the maze.

Nobody tried to put a really interesting reward at the end of the maze, to see if that would make the rats run faster, or figure out the maze a whole lot quicker than the electro-shocked rats had. Or if the happy rats remembered the maze better ... acted more intelligently all around ...

Well.

I can tell you from personal experience that the happy rats would have easily outperformed the freaked out, stressed rats at -5, which is supposed to be "optimum performance," every time and with consummate ease.

Effortlessly.

Elegantly.

Most of all, **predictably**.

All Stress Is Bad Stress

Remember we started out with my past aspects investigating "rage syndrome" in domesticated animals?

When creatures seem to go mad "for no good reason" and will attack anything and anyone in their immediate environment?

Well, the whole idea that "some stress is good for you" and the old Yerkes-Dobson "law" has persisted because *it seems* that stressed creatures are more active and perform better than relaxed creatures.

There are higher activity levels as stress increases, this is true. Mice start scurrying and people's thoughts start racing. Their hearts start pumping faster to prepare for "fight or flight" - for an EMERGENCY SITUATION.

As we are totally unused to seeing domesticated animals and fellow human beings perform at the positive high energy levels, it seems that there is "more being done" when stress sets in, people are starting to run around like headless chickens and energy levels are getting lower and lower.

This gives us the crazed day traders, screaming insanely into their telephones and dropping dead of heart attacks, having mental, physical and emotional meltdowns and "burn out" at an early age as a direct result.

Please hear this.

There is no such thing as good stress. All stress is very bad for you.

Stressing is for short time real life and death emergency situations ONLY - when the worst has already happened, and we're throwing our last resources into the battle in a final act of desperation.

This is neither good, nor beneficial in any way, not for anyone. Not even for a general, throwing their last troops into a desperate fight. Even there, the soldiers, if they were on the right side of the SUE Scale, would outperform the stressed out enemy physically, mentally, emotionally - and especially in the long run.

It doesn't matter if you're trading shares, patrolling in enemy territory, trying to get your kids to school, sell double glazing or create a beautiful piece of programming - stress is bad for you, it will wreck your performance, and high energy individuals will trump you every single time.

This is worth knowing, worth remembering, and worth passing on!

There really is no such thing as "good stress."
If it's good, it wasn't stress. It was excitement instead.

The Pyramid Model Of Modern Stress Management

Here is my replacement for the "Hebbian Stress Curve" which had falsely put "optimum performance" at serious stress of -5.

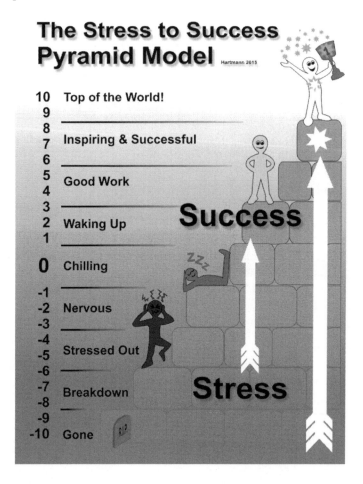

This is a far more accurate and complete description of what happens to people in mind, body and spirit when their energy levels change.

Below Zero, a person will become consecutively more stressed, more nervous, more anxious, more paranoid, more confused, more incapable of clear thought and congruent action.

This gets worse until the crisis point is reached at -8. That's the state where the final flare up occurs - the complete psychotic break, "rage syndrome," total loss of control.

This version of the energy chart is simple, logical and you can apply this practically in your real life, as we shall see.

From The Old To The New

I don't know how much scientific entrainment you've gone through, dear reader, but I'm asking you now, adult human being to adult human being, do you want to put your trust, your faith and your future into the industry standard Yerkes-Dobson rat model from 1908?

Do you want to gamble the success, the mental and physical health of your family, your children, your company and your country on a reality deficient, deeply flawed and entirely outdated model that has failed us all spectacularly for over a hundred years now?

I would also ask, is it any wonder at all that for all the rise in global expenditure on stress management programs there are no significant beneficial results?

Is it any wonder that the world is getting more and more stressed - if the one and only "law" is driving folks deeper into stress, rather than bringing them out of it?

- **Putting "optimum performance" at -5 (instead of at +10, where it rightfully belongs!) is the <u>direct cause</u> for the failure of existing stress management programs.**

It is also the direct cause for general stupidity, small mindedness, greed, "dog eat dog" mentality and so many other nasty side effects that are plaguing our modern society.

Everyone's singing of the same hymn sheet.

The 1908 "let's shock the rats" hymn sheet.

You question that, and you're "unscientific."

Because Yerkes-Dobson is "THE LAW of arousal."

And I am right back with that behaviourist back in the day.

"You know I'm right about this! What is wrong with you???"

"If you think I'm going to change all my handouts manuals I've spent 40 years writing, you've got another thing coming!"

EVERYONE is singing off the same hymn sheet.

Everyone in the business of stress management would need to re-write their handouts manuals if the SUE Scale came out, and was adopted.

Nobody wants to do that.

Nobody wants to rock the boat.

So here we are once more.

I have the solution to the problem.

I have a clear cut, logical theoretical model that makes sense.

41

This model produces practical, easy, cost effective strategies to lead out of stress, and into success.

It would make people's lives happier.

It would make any company which applies it more profitable.

It would make the kids in any school where the teachers and students learned about this brighter, smarter, stronger, faster and more effective in love, life, work and play.

It would save the various health insurance companies and government sponsored health care programs billions upon billions in having to treat the aftermath of a population driven ever deeper into stress.

But hey ...

"If you think I'm going to re-write my manuals, you've got another thing coming ..."

There have been a few improvements since 1908.

It's time to upgrade to

The 2015 version of Modern Stress Management.

So now, I am appealing to you directly, dear reader.

I am appealing to you as a human being, a real living person, someone who has intelligence, common sense, but most of all, the experience of your own life to draw upon.

I am not asking you to take my word for it.

I am asking you to start observing how people behave, with the Energy Chart and the SUE Scale in mind.

I am asking you start noticing how entire tribes, societies, countries, companies show the entirely predictable signs of stress.

I am asking you personally to start a movement, out of the old cage that ended at Zero, into that whole new landscape on the POSITIVE side of the SUE Scale.

Try it out for yourself.

After decades of trying to get folk to listen, I've come to this conclusion.

We cannot wait for a government, a leader, "science" or the second coming of Christ - some authority who waves a magic wand and the old is gone, the new is finally here.

There is stress, there are vested interests, there is fear and inertia. All of that is on the wrong side of Zero and a direct result of everyone being way too stressed.

The only way forward is for individuals to "get it" how it works, to try it out for themselves, learn for themselves what's right and what's wrong (I call that "wisdom learning").

Then they can tell others about this.

Especially people in power over other people, such as mothers, fathers, teachers, managers and CEOs must step forward and adopt that move into the right direction, out of stress and towards the unknown realms of real success, one by one.

It's critically important for any individual, and for humanity at large, that we should start to become ...

Master Of Emotions

In 2001, an excited gentleman suggested we should write a book together. Actually, I should write the book, and he would market it - we could share the profits.

The book was to be called, "Master Your Emotions" and the excited gentleman had a book on EFT (Emotional Freedom Techniques) in mind.

I started with the project, but it soon dawned on me that just EFT wasn't really the answer.

It wasn't by itself and certainly not at that time.

Mastering your emotions isn't just about "tapping bad emotions away so you don't have to have them any longer."

Mastering your emotions isn't even about being able to move up and down the SUE scale at will by tapping EFT, either on negative statements, or on positive ones.

- **Mastering emotions requires a totally different approach, a more natural, logical way to deal with energy movements in the real world, in real time, in real response to the real challenges of this life.**

I believe that humanity has had the problems it has had (and still has) with emotions because the people who are doing the thinking, the philosophy, religion and the science on behalf of all humanity were ... men.

Take your basic idea of the Great Oriental Zen Master who can slay an enemy just by looking at them, take down 45 men armed with axes in combat, and is "in total control of their emotions."

By having a totally blank face, no matter what the weather ...

For a long time, I thought, well, perhaps they do master their emotions eventually, and that's what you end up with. Stony faced, that's what enlightenment looks like ...

But then, I saw a movie.

It was quite modern, 21st Century and featured an imaginary modern day Great Oriental Master type, who was ever so good at kicking people in the head and whirling staffs around.

His family dies in a car crash, his wife and kids.

And how does the great martial arts master and so called energy (chi) expert deal with this significant emotional experience ..?

By ...

a) being totally miserable, angry, depressed, withdrawn and lonely all year long;

b) spending all his time as soon as he comes home from work repairing the actual car his wife and kids died in, and

c) on the anniversary of their deaths/the car crash, taking a baseball bat to the car and destroying it, so he can spend another bitter, miserable year re-building it yet again so it's ready to be smashed on the next anniversary afresh.

This was a very popular movie that undoubtedly, millions of young oriental boys and Western boys too watched wide eyed in their admiration.

OK ... and so that's our oriental 21st Century role model for .... ahm ... "emotional mastery" ...?

My ass!

That's pathetic.

That's pathological.

Go see a psychologist, at great speed ...

Oh, I forgot. That won't help. The psychologists don't have a definition for emotions, nor any workable methods how to change them.

That's because "the fathers of psychology" were all men.

And men are entrained to "not have emotions" from an early age.

To consider emotions a sign of weakness and failure, and leave them to the women.

Well, of course, men have emotions.

But they try to ignore them as best they can, and are taught to *pretend they don't have them*.

The better you are at pretending, the more like that Great Oriental Zen Master you can pretend to be, the more money you win at poker ... or something like that ...

But hear this.

You can't master anything you don't understand.

You certainly cannot master anything that you ignore, and at the final frontier, *you can't master something you're pretending doesn't even exist*.

In order to master your emotions,
you need to understand emotions.

That is the absolute 101 of anything, and it is true, I was totally astonished when I found that there was no working definition in any field of existing science as to what "emotions" are when they're at home.

45

The only thing I did find was people trying to not have any emotions at all, in order to do "good science."

Oh, but what an epic fail that has proven to be!

If you've ever spent any time around scientists, you'll probably notice that they are far from unemotional.

Mr Spock, where are you ...?

Scientists are very emotional.

Especially the ones who really love science and the idea of no emotions.

They literally start foaming at the mouth and screaming abuse when you come in with the notion that we actually really do have an energy body, and that this energy body transmits feedback signals through the physical body.

The energy body produces "sensations" through the 6th sense.

That those sensations are emotions. That we need them in the same way we need to experience physical sensations, to keep us safe, happy and healthy in our lives here on Earth.

It couldn't be simpler.

So I really have to ask - what were those oriental monks doing for 6,000 years in their monasteries, undisturbed by women and children, or any kind of real life?

Standing around on one leg, pretending to be cranes? Snakes?

What a useless lot, and what a waste of time.

Yet it all comes down and back to this "trying to ignore emotions" deal.

Trying to get by on a reduced reality model where there is no such thing as energy.

And it doesn't work.

If you don't believe me, switch on the news.

Hear of all the crises - financial, environmental, adversarial, interpersonal.

The "world of men" is a mess.

It's a mess because men have ignored emotions.

Simple.

Now, if you're a man, don't get upset.

It's not your fault.

You were brought up in the old, as was I.

We were both raised in stress induced insanity, with no way out.

Actually, it's worse.

If you put "Zero emotions" as the best it can get, that's the end.

We are trapped in a horrendous prison of stress, misery and deprivation, and we don't even look for a way out!

That's probably the greatest tragedy.

And it is so insane, because every real person I've ever spoken to, men, women, children, teenagers, old folk alike, everyone does have experiences of GOOD emotional states.

They're just being completely ignored by pathological science.

47

But here's the good news.

- **By paying more attention to our positive emotional states we can learn a lot about how to get a hold of emotions in general.**

Emotions are simply feedback devices to how the energy system is working.

That's it.

They're not demons, they're not some mad thing from out of nowhere.

Above all else, we're not "making them up" and they're definitely not "all in your mind."

Emotions are direct, simple, and when we understand that and embrace it, we're nearly there and we can begin a journey into true emotional mastery that is exciting and hugely beneficial.

Beneficial for each one of us, but more so, for all the poor souls who have to deal with us!

So let's get practical now and discuss some ways in which we can put my structurally correct model of emotions to work in order to eventually, truly become the masters of emotion.

Learn Yourself!

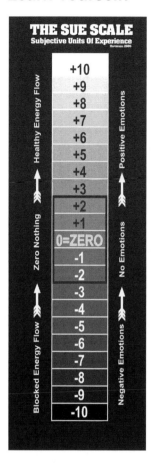

THE SUE SCALE
Subjective Units Of Experience

Healthy Energy Flow — Positive Emotions

Zero Nothing — No Emotions

Blocked Energy Flow — Negative Emotions

+10
+9
+8
+7
+6
+5
+4
+3
+2
+1
0=ZERO
-1
-2
-3
-4
-5
-6
-7
-8
-9
-10

The first step to emotional mastery is to **learn yourself.**

Learn how you work as a living system, and what you do at the various levels of energy flow.

Important:

As we become more stressed, have less and less energy, and our systems react to this with panic, fear and anxiety, we start to lose the ability to get out of stress by ourselves.

We literally "lose the plot" below -5.

We lose control over the system; I think of this as being on a stress river that's going towards a major waterfall and you didn't get to the bank and safety while you still could.

Above -5, you can still get yourself out of stress by doing something that re-energizes you; if you let it slip below that, you're in big trouble.

* If there's someone around who also knows this scale and can help you, stabilise you, give you energy at that point, this slide down into insanity can still be reversed.

What we need to learn now is to re-connect our emotions and feelings, our thoughts and behaviours (our actions, what we do), back together into a single working totality.

When we do that, we can learn to understand ourselves.

We can understand why we think and act the way we do.

That is the first step to developing an urgent desire to make changes, to have a better life, to be higher, more often.

To get out of stress, and into success.

Let's have a look at how the Energy Chart affects some of the things we deal with on an every day basis.

49

The World According To SUE

Energy state changes are the causal influence that decides how we think, feel and act.

When we are energized, we think, feel and act completely differently compared to being low on energy, being on the minus side of the Stress Chart.

At -6, everyone starts to stutter.

At +6, everyone is smiling.

It is extraordinary how this simple cause and effect in people has been so overlooked, so misinterpreted, and for so long.

A person said to me once, "I can't believe how the world changes when I am happier in myself."

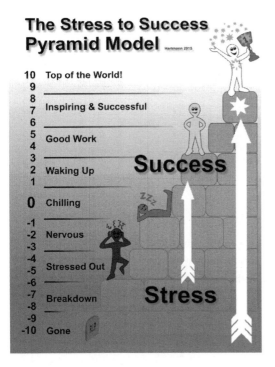

The lights are brighter. Gravity is lighter. Colours are more radiant, and tastes and scents as well as sensations become heightened, become *sensational.*

That's the tip of the iceberg.

People change from "introvert" to "extrovert." People change their minds. They change their beliefs.

Everything **changes when we change state, when we change the levels of energy in our energy bodies.**

Here are some examples how the world changes, depending on your energy body stress levels at the time.

Here is a brief reminder of the Energy Chart, and now let's take a look at how this practically manifests.

Self Esteem & Confidence

The extraordinary fact is that each and every person thinks, feels and believes completely different things about everything - depending where they are on the Energy Chart. This is an example of a perfectly ordinary young woman and "self esteem, confidence and body image."

-10	
-9	
-8	The world would be better off without me - I wish I was dead.
-7	I am a hideous monstrosity.
-6	I am horribly ugly
-5	*Everything* about me is wrong.
-4	My nose is too big, my breasts too small and my bottom is enormous.
-3	I don't like the way I look.
-2	Not looking my best today.
-1	It will have to do ...
0	I am ordinary.
+1	I guess I look OKish ...
+2	Not too bad today ...
+3	I look alright
+4	My hair looks nice today
+5	I quite like the way I look
+6	I am quite good looking
+7	I like the way I look
+8	I am beautiful
+9	I am really beautiful, I like myself!
+10	I am perfect and exactly right and I feel great!

There are essentially two ways to go from here.

You can either enter therapy and try to "permanently fix my self esteem so I will never feel ugly again," and good luck with that.

Or you can learn how to raise your energy to get on the right side of the SUE scale, at any time you need this, and there it is - eternal beauty, eternal youth, just for the taking.

51

I would suggest you make your own "confidence and body image" chart and write down, in black and white, for you to see what happens to you when your energy drops.

- What do you think and say at the different energy levels?
- What do you always think, say and feel when your energy is high?
- What do you always think, say and feel when your energy is low?
- What do you always think you have to do, depending on your energy levels?

What is so important here is to realise that whatever you are thinking and feeling is just a reflection of your energy body state.

Instead of thinking your way out of a problem, for example, simply raise energy. Then your thinking will work much better and you will find the solution.

Now we may ask, how do we raise energy?

Everyone has their ways, and it's important that we become aware of the ways we already use to bring our energy levels up.

For example, pay attention to what you do to "make yourself feel more confident" and how that is working for you.

My art project friend, the business man, was using his extraordinarily expensive watch as an "anchor" to remind himself that he was a successful man.

I could see how he would glance at it, not to tell the time, but to centre himself and raise energy. He did this a lot. If he had consciously known that this was what he was doing, he could have stepped into that process with volition and raised more energy, and raised it higher.

I knew a young man once who bought clothes by a particular designer, even though they were super-expensive and he really could not afford them. But as soon as he put on those designer clothes, it would raise his energy and he would "be more confident."

Yet another young man would walk proud and confidently when he was wearing a tailored suit - but put him in a pair of shorts and a T-shirt, he would slouch and become shy, lose his confidence.

A suit is just cloth, just the same as a T-Shirt is cloth. I suggested he should walk "as though he was wearing a suit" - and he transformed. His energy unfolded, he started to smile, stand up straighter, breathe more deeply.

An invisible "power suit" doesn't stain, doesn't crinkle, doesn't cost a dime. No-one can take it away from you. And you are free to choose your clothes in a whole new way.

Once you consciously realise that what you are doing is purely designed to raise your energy, you gain control over all manner of things.

To start with, just notice the cause and effect of your thoughts, behaviours, feelings and your energy levels in your own life. That's the very first step.

Business & Work Success

-10	
-9	
-8	The world would be better off without me - I wish I was dead.
-7	I am the eternal loser ...
-6	I am such a loser.
-5	*Everything* I do goes wrong.
-4	I can't make this work, it's too hard.
-3	I must work harder, I must get this sorted, get this under control.
-2	Lots of work to do and never enough time.
-1	Work sucks but I have to get on with it.
0	It's just work.
+1	Work is okish ...
+2	Not too bad today ...
+3	I quite enjoy my work.
+4	I am good at my work.
+5	I am successful.
+6	I enjoy work.
+7	I really enjoy my work.
+8	I love my work - it's awesome!
+9	I absolutely love what I'm doing - this is it!
+10	The whole world is at my fingertips!

Whenever we see one of these Energy Charts, it is really mind blowing to contemplate that **this is the same person** thinking, feeling, being all these different people.

It is amazing that a single person can go from "I hold the whole world in my hand!" to "I am the greatest loser of all time!" in a single day, in fact, in a split second.

But it happens. And it happens more often, the more highly intelligent, highly creative any given person already is. For creative people, these huge swings up and down the Energy Chart happen all the time, on a daily basis.

This is strongly exacerbated by substance abuse. Substance highs, followed by their inevitable major lows as the energy system tries to recover make these so called "mood swings" worse and more extreme over time.

To understand clearly that it isn't some mysterious "mood" that swings, but that it is the energy body reacting to what's happening, is of the essence on so many different levels.

Trying to run a successful business, or to be consistently successful at work, becomes a totally different ball game when you are energy aware.

Clearly, and very importantly, *do not **ever** make important decisions when you are too low on the Energy Chart.*

As we have observed, your field of vision collapses into smaller and smaller details, until very bad decisions are being taken that will cause even more problems in the future. The classic example of this is how people under high stress will take out shark loans with thousands of percent interest, or credit cards to fix their financial problems.

Obviously, you should also never try to give a presentation to an important customer, write kick ass marketing materials, make that marriage proposal, choose the colour palette of your bedroom or do anything important when you are too stressed.

Modern energy work offers a simple and sustainable alternative to having to snort a few lines of coke in order to "get it on."

From the other point of view, handling "temperamental" creatives becomes oh so much easier and more logical once you've understood the energy chart.

Becoming energy aware can quite practically stop the very best people from self destruction, burn out and insanity.

Indeed, it can give these people a way forward to accessing levels of creativity, intelligence, and perfection in logic that they have always dreamed and hoped to reach one day.

It is breathtaking to contemplate the effects the simple Energy Chart can have on the performance of people on every level of work and business. Entrepreneurs especially really need to sit down and sort out their unique personal stress charts.

Success in business absolutely relies on being on the right side of zero.

Goals, Hopes & Dreams

-10	
-9	
-8	I can't stand this any longer - make it all stop!
-7	I wish the whole world would go up in flames!
-6	I am losing the war I'm in!
-5	I am at war!
-4	I must protect everything myself.
-3	I must keep it together somehow.
-2	It's OK now but it's only going to get worse.
-1	It's OK as it is, I guess.
0	I am at peace.
+1	I might do something today.
+2	I would quite like to do something today.
+3	I am going to do something good today.
+4	I am going to do something - right now!
+5	I am doing something to further the future.
+6	I know exactly what I'm doing and why.
+7	I am creating reality!
+8	I am creating reality - and this is fun!
+9	I am living my life - and it's awesome!
+10	I am the master of my destiny and my vision.

This is our single person again, from anywhere in the world, in different states, and these different states cause different thoughts, behaviours and actions.

They also change values, beliefs and attitudes.

From these different states, different "goals, hopes and dreams" come into being.

Basically, if you spend enough time around -7, you too will become the evil genius who wants to destroy the whole world. It's structural and systemic. Which means that, with an energy chart in hand, you get to choose if you want to be a superhero or a super villain. If you want to be good, or evil.

Just how "conservative" you want to be, or how "progressive" (or liberal!).

55

You will also be able to tell where other people spend most of their incarnation, which states they inhabit most often.

Indeed, as we have observed, we can plot entire civilisations according to SUE.

Further, it makes perfect sense that if you can make people angry/unhappy/energy deprived enough, they will normally and naturally turn into bloodthirsty, raving lunatics, terrorists and mass murderers. It's easy.

"Tell my your goal, and I tell you who you are."

What particularly annoys me personally is the idea that we can all get together at Zero, and "make peace."

You could imagine that it's the "middle ground" on the Energy Chart, and the folks from -7 can meet the folks from +7, and they can shake hands in the no-mans-land of Zero, feeling nothing at all, and we can all live happily, no, emotion free that would be, ever after ...

That's insanity.

It will never work.

"Peace" is a death goal.

My partner describes it as "trying to balance on a see-saw, precariously, and you relax for an instance, and you fall right off again."

The place to meet is on the other side of the energy chart.

Indeed, we can't even "meet" properly, make a connection with our energy bodies and create a group bubble where information and energy is exchanged, until we're at least at a +5.

All of us together.

I would put the meeting point for humanity at +10, myself.

There, we really will become "one."

We really will understand each other.

Forgive each other.

LOVE each other.

Let's set the goal posts not higher, but *righter.*

Forget about peace.

Make love your goal.

Questions

-10	
-9	
-8	Why does God hate me?
-7	What's wrong with me?
-6	What have I done wrong?
-5	Where am I going wrong?
-4	What's going wrong?
-3	What's going on here?
-2	There's something not quite right ...
-1	I don't really have any questions.
0	I have no questions.
+1	I don't really have any questions ...
+2	There might be something good to come?
+3	Where is something good?
+4	I am going to get me some of that good stuff.
+5	I've got the good stuff - now, where's better?
+6	I've got the better stuff - where's even better than that?
+7	Wow! This is fantastic!
+8	There's more than I ever thought there was ...
+9	This is mind blowing - I can explore everything ...
+10	There are no questions, only actions :-)

Whilst working with the SUE scale and every day occurrences, with all sorts of people, we became aware of the fact that if you're high, you are not really asking the usual kinds of questions any longer.

For example, there was a one-man-band business owner who had been asking the same question for a decade - "How can I get more people to come to my business?"

This question would always generate the answers. The usual answers, the usual suspects. "Do more advertising. Do more marketing. Work harder. Get on the phones. Work harder. Harder, harder, harder ..."

He took this for granted and enacted this; and his business really didn't make that much progress over the same decade that the same question was being asked, and the exact same answers always arrived, followed by the exact same pattern of frantic, stressed, energy deprived (aka unattractive!) activity.

Then, he became aware of the Energy Chart and when the business took a dive, as they do, he said, "I actually heard myself ask that same old question.

"I decided to stop and do something energizing first, to find out if I would get different answers.

"But that didn't happen. Instead, I stopped asking the question altogether and did something!"

That's the key to understanding questions in relationship to the Energy Chart.

We will always ask the same stress driven questions when we get low on energy, and it doesn't matter if you're a theoretical physicist or a pole dancer.

These stress driven questions produce stress driven answers, followed by stress driven activities - and none of that "solves the problem."

In fact, the very fact that we're sitting there, asking these (stupid) questions yet again, such as ...

> *Why doesn't anybody love me?*
>
> *How do I get more customers?*
>
> *How do I get more visitors to my web site?*
>
> *How do I get laid more often?*
>
> *What do I have to do to lose weight?*
>
> *What's wrong with me ...?*

... well, those questions are yet again, nothing more than the red light flashing on our metaphorical dashboard to tell you that you are stressed!

Back in the day when I was playing the old psychology game, and took it for granted that you have to go back into your childhood, solve a trauma, and then you'll never feel (unsuccessful, unloved, unwanted, hopeless, idea-less) ever again, I became aware that **questions are <u>generators</u> of answers**.

Endless generators. And I mean endless. Infinite.

You can ask that question of, "What's wrong with me?" and each one of us can spend the rest of our lives doing nothing else but compile a list of everything that's wrong with any of us.

I was then looking for a way to get myself and other people off of this endless treadmill of stress crazy questions that generate endless further depressing answers - and of course, the answer was to stop it with the old Freudian nonsense, and instead, start thinking energy.

The fact is that we would never ask stupid questions if we weren't so stressed.

We'd be DOING something instead.

Something proactive, something fun - living life, working, playing, being in the flow.

The next time, you're with some person, and they look at you all teary eyed and whisper, "What's wrong with me ...?" you can smile at them and tell them, "You are stressed. That's what's wrong with you, and that is ALL that's wrong with you."

Under the topic of "Learn yourself!" please do take a moment and round up your personal great "life's questions."

Write them down on a piece of paper and consider what kind of low energy state the person who would be asking such a question has to be at.

Then burn the piece of paper, get some fresh air, raise your energy and DO whatever needs to be done to move your incarnation forward to the next level.

Life becomes far more natural, and far more satisfying when we begin to understand that **questions are an indication of low energy flow**.

The answers are, as are all good things, on the positive side of the SUE scale.

They are, to be sure, answers to very different questions than those the stressed mind will be asking.

But that's a good thing too.

I'm sure we're all quite aware that although a brand new super car would be a very nice toy, it's not "the answer to everything."

:-)

Emotions & Feelings

-10	
-9	
-8	I can't stand this any longer - make it all stop!
-7	I must cause myself so much physical pain that I can't feel the other pain anymore.
-6	I'm in terrible pain.
-5	Feeling like this is awful.
-4	I feel bad.
-3	I don't feel right.
-2	I feel sort of numb.
-1	Not feeling much.
0	I feel nothing. Empty. Pointless.
+1	Not feeling much.
+2	I feel alright, I guess.
+3	I feel OK.
+4	I'm feeling optimistic.
+5	I feel good.
+6	I feel really good.
+7	I feel great!
+8	I feel awesome!
+9	Wow! I am amazed how fantastic I feel!
+10	Words can't describe this. It's a miracle.

Emotions and feelings are of course, the big "no go" zone of humanity. Men are supposed to be in that straight jacket around the Zero point of nothingness, but of course, they're not.

They do try though with all their might because they want to be "a good, strong, powerful man," and succeed only in disconnecting from the very feedback systems that would help them achieve this. Those who succeed in becoming disconnected from their own 6th Sense sensations are very bitter to discover that it didn't make them any more popular, rich, powerful or sexually attractive at all in the end ...

60

Women are allowed to have more freedom of energy movements, up and down the Energy Chart. Indeed, if you don't howl like a banshee for at least a fortnight at the top of your lungs, you probably weren't a very good wife and you didn't love your dead husband enough ...

It's a crazy, crazy world we have inherited here from the venerable ancestors.

Personally, I was never that interested in feminism or women's rights. I was always more interested in how *people* work.

I figured that if I can figure that out, then I'll know how women work AND how men work, and we can find some common ground.

Although men and women have of course different energy bodies, everybody's energy body is very different from everyone else's.

If you think your DNA makes you special, or your fingerprints, you've seen nothin' yet ...

Energy bodies are unique from the moment of conception, and every single thing that happens after that makes them more and more unique.

In the old ancestor worshipping, samey cultures everything possible was done to curtail this intense individualisation. Making everyone have the same thoughts, hear the same words, speak the same words in the same way, sing the same songs, have the same experiences at the same age in the same order, perform the exact same actions and (try to) have the exact same lives as the ancestors who went before them is an effort in that direction.

That didn't even work back in the day of huts and villages; nowadays, it's utterly and completely hopeless.

So we try and make every girl look like the latest fashion icon, and every boy look like the currently trendy pop star, and there's plastic surgery and all of that, but still, that intense individualisation of the energy body will out ...

Truth will out, as they say.

And it comes out in emotions and feelings, and the behaviours that are driven by those feelings and emotions.

Behaviours such as art and war, drug abuse, religious fanaticism, philosophy, song, tale, movie, fashion, politics, banking and all that jazz ...

Anyone who doesn't understand that the human world runs on emotion is a fool.

A dangerous fool.

There is simply no other word for it.

They are a dangerous fool because they're mired deeply on the wrong side of the Energy Chart, to be sure - but a fool, and dangerous, nonetheless.

We need to take a totally different stance on emotions.

First of all, we - as a species! - need to acknowledge that we have emotions.

We get angry, we get sad. We fall in love. Anyone who doesn't have emotions is not normal, not a normal human being. They are sick, pathological in some way,

61

and need care and good treatment rather than perversely being admired for this and held up as role models to anyone at all.

We need to stop pretending that we are in control of emotions when this is simply not true.

Let's get real.

Please.

That's the first step in the right direction.

Once we - all 6 billion of us! - sat in a big circle and acknowledged the fact that we have emotions, we can all take a big sigh of relief, all together and at the same time.

The cat's out of the bag. Or the rat is out of the maze, as the case may be ...

It's a start.

Now we can start talking about when we are having emotions, and when we do that, we discover how emotions work.

That's what I've been doing.

My whole life long I've been asking people about their experiences, about their emotions, and creating a space where they could tell me how they felt when x, y and z happened.

How they feel now when they think about v, w, and u.

Yes, that's what I did.

And by doing that for a few decades, I finally found the Guiding Stars and the other important events in people's lives, and learned that we are not defined by trauma, no matter how traumatic life might have been.

- **True emotional mastery starts with understanding emotions, and in order to understand emotions, you have to understand the energy body.**

Please be advised, when I say "understanding the energy body" I do NOT mean spending the next 30 years studying ancient, outmoded, useless models full of arbitrary points and lines, made up by some guys in sandals some 6,000 years ago.

I mean YOUR LIVING ENERGY BODY. Right here, right now.

Yours, mine, his and hers.

The reality of how emotion works, how it manifests, and how we can change emotions.

In order to understand emotions, you have to understand energy.

It's not difficult.

Once you've seen it somewhere in action, you all of sudden see it everywhere.

Yes, and I guess that's what they mean by "enlightenment."

Easy.

62

Unsubtle Energy

We need to be quite clear that when I talk about energy, I am not talking about the New Age idea of "subtle energy."

Energy isn't subtle.

Our energy bodies are not subtle.

They are primal, powerful, and they run our lives via our emotions from the cradle to the grave.

When a man whose wife of 60 years has died, also dies within the year, that's not subtle. That's "dying of a broken heart" and people are doing it all the time.

When a man beats his wife to a pulp because he can't control his "anger," that's not subtle.

When someone jumps off a motorway bridge because they can't stand the emotional pain any longer, and thus causes a massive pile up in which a further 40 people are burned alive, and another 200 need to be ferried into the hospitals, that's not subtle.

When a terrorist straps a bomb to themselves and blows themselves up, taking a whole restaurant of people with them, that's not subtle.

When a boy brings an arsenal to school and shoots his teachers and fellow pupils, that's not subtle.

When a country goes to war with another country, because of fear and hatred, that's not subtle.

When one people put another people into concentration camps and tortures and kills them by their millions, that's not subtle.

And when billions of people all at the same time are driven deeper and deeper into stress, paranoia and insanity on mass, that's definitely not "subtle."

The talk of "subtle energy" must cease.

It's a misunderstanding, a misinterpretation, an aberration that leads people away from the brutal reality of the true cost of energy body disturbances in our lives, in our civilisations.

Energy may be invisible, immeasurable, lighter than light - but its effects on all of us are absolutely extraordinary.

So let's forget about "subtle energy" and instead, let's focus on real energy.

Where do you feel that (love, hatred, fear, terror, panic) in your body?
Show me with your hands ...

Mapping People

People are not as complicated as we used to think they are.

Everyone has different thoughts, questions, goals, behaviours, actions, even different values at different SUE levels.

You can be nice and naughty, insane and very logical, a genius and a total fool all in the same day, *sequentially* - and we all are.

That's just being human.

What we need to learn is to **map people with the energy body stress chart in mind.**

This starts with and includes ourselves, of course.

I would like to offer you a simple model which I have found to be very useful when it comes to understanding people - and our ourselves.

The Aspects Model

We are not just "one person."

"What kind of person" we are depends on our energy body stress levels.

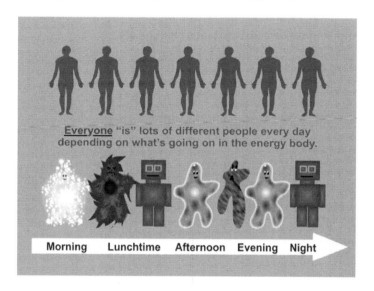

Every one of us can be at least 21 different people, if we use the SUE Scale as a guide.

This happens sequentially, meaning that you can never be nice and nasty at the same time; one follows after the other.

For example.

Peter is feeling great, so he's nice to his wife, buys her a gift, is happy. On the way home, he gets into a car accident that wasn't his fault. The shock causes his energy system to go down fast, into -7, and he flies into road rage and beats up the other driver. The police drags him away in handcuffs ...

Is Peter nice, or is he nasty? Is he sane, or is he insane? Is he a good man, or a bad man? A good citizen or a criminal?

This basic problem of trying to label a person to be one thing, or the other, and that is "who they are" lies at the root of a multitude of sins.

In order to sort this out, I proposed that we talk of any "Peter" who isn't here, right now, as "an aspect."

The same works for ourselves - instead of saying, "I wet my pants when I was three years old," we say, "My three year old aspect wet their pants."

65

That makes a whole lot more sense, and allows for the reality that we can be "different people" - *depending on our energy states at the time*.

The simple use of the Aspects Model makes human relationships inordinately easier, and far more logical.

When we say, "My aspect was stressed to insanity," we have a more logical way to address this. We can ask what happened, we can learn from it.

We can also then go on to apply this to other people.

Instead of saying, "My partner is an idiot," we can say, "The aspect who did that was an idiot."

What we will find, time and time again, is that *aspects do bad things when they're stressed*.

When they're not stressed, they don't.

And ... when they're energy high, they do *wonderful* things.

We are capable of doing wonderful things.

We all are.

We can have future aspects who can do things that we, here and now, can't even conceive of as yet.

And it's all just a matter of energy.

Pay With Attention, Buy Happiness

If you want to start on your own personal journey of emotional mastery, start with the SUE scale in hand, and use it to assess people - including yourself! - as you go through your normal, daily life.

Don't try and make any changes yet, simply notice how people go up and down on the SUE scale all day long as their energy rises and falls.

Importantly, notice how they become "better people" when they are more energized (happier) and "worse people" when their energy drops below Zero (unhappier).

Start to notice how people at various stress levels say and do things in very predictable ways - and how this changes when energy levels change, also predictably.

For example, you might have a friend who immediately starts to whine about their husband when stress levels are low. When the same friend is energized, their husband can do no wrong and is much loved and admired.

Notice what causes "stress spikes" in your own reality - for you, for other people.

It's simply fascinating to match up the model with what you can see, feel, hear and sense around you.

And it's the only way for you to not just believe what I'm telling you to be the truth, but to actually understand how it all works from the inside out.

Once you "see it," the world will never be the same again.

It will become safer, more predictable, more logical in every way.

We can start to answer our oldest questions.

"What's wrong with him?!?!?!?" - "He's stressed, he's at -7, about to go completely insane ..."

"Why is she always changing her mind like the weather?!?!?!?" - "She's moving up and down on the SUE Scale fast and often, she's very reactive. Different SUE states, different opinions ..."

"Are we humans born bad?!?!?!?" - "Nope. Just conceived, carried to term and born into a cauldron of stress ..."

"Why are people so stupid?!?!?!?" - "They're not. They're just stressed. If you de-stress them, re-energize them, they'll become much, much smarter. Try it out, it's true!"

"Why does nobody love me?!?!?!?" - "First of all, be aware, you wouldn't even be thinking that if you weren't so stressed! You need to energize, fast! Secondly, people who are low on energy are energy suckers, not energy givers. You want them to love you, you need to raise their energy first so they've got some love to give to you!"

"What's wrong with me?!?!?" - "You are stressed. You need to move up on the SUE Scale so you stop asking a question that is an endless generator of more and more answers as to "what's wrong with you" - and will lead you into more and more and more stress!"

Energy makes sense.

It makes sense of the world (of people).

Without factoring energy into the equation, it doesn't resolve.

But when you add "energy awareness," all of a sudden even the most extraordinary insanity that people are capable of starts to make perfect sense.

This is the big breakthrough - simply understanding how it works.

Once a person has understood the Stress Chart, the rest pretty much can take of itself.

If this is all news to you, give yourself a week or so.

Carry the stress chart with you, in your pocket, wherever you go, and whatever you do. Wear a SUE wristband and check your energy levels at least as often as you would check a watch, or your mobile phone for important messages.

Even when you're just sitting on the couch, watching TV, have your stress chart to hand. How are your energy levels, your activity levels, your life levels reacting to what you're seeing/hearing/experiencing there?

An advertisement winds you up - notice that drop that's making you angry, that's making you say angry things, having angry thoughts and angry feelings in your body.

An advertisement turns you on - notice how it raises your energy, how that's making you think different things, feel different things in your body.

In other words, ***start paying attention to yourself.***

In energy terms, "paying with attention" always results in getting something valuable in return.

Information, above all else.

The higher you are on the SUE Scale, the more information becomes available to you, and the more you can do with that information.

It's fascinating, and well worth playing with, in your own time.

Taking Control Of Your Energy States

After observing yourself and other people for a while, the desire rises to take charge and do something to avoid the miserable states below Zero that make you weak, annoying, clumsy, unlucky, stupid and sick. Now, we can ask the question - HOW DO WE RAISE ENERGY?

First, the good news. You don't have to twist yourself like a pretzel in Yoga for the next 20 years, nor do you have to study Buddhism or become a Scientologist.

Raising energy is really, really easy. Let me give you an example.

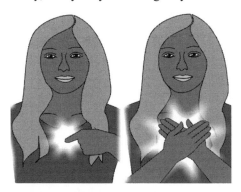

First, have a look at this SUE Scale and notice where you are at this time.

Slide your finger across it until it feels about right. Got a number? Excellent.

Now, point to the place on your chest where you would point to say, "I, this is me!" Place the palm of your leading hand so it covers that spot, then place your other hand on top of that.

We call this **The Heart Position**. You are putting your hands on your heart of energy or energy heart, the centre of your energy body.

Take a moment to become aware of the sensations of your own hands on your chest, and then take three deep breaths, in and out. You can breathe in fresh air and breathe out worries and problems if you want to.

Now, take another deep breath, and **think of something or someone you love.**

Think about that. Keep breathing in and out deeply with your hands on your heart and by all means, let any sensations of loving this (X) rise up and become stronger. Take another three deep breaths.

Now, check the SUE Scale. Also note how you are feeling inside (6th sense, this is how "you feel.")

If you thought of something you really love, and it doesn't matter if that was your cat, your dream car, a sexy movie star or your favourite grandchild, chances are, your energy has risen.

You feel happier in yourself, less stressed, far more relaxed.

This is a simple, basic principle of "modern energy work."

- **We become happier (less stressed) when we move towards something positive, beautiful, beneficial, desirable, something we love. That takes us higher on the energy body chart.**

- **We become unhappier (more stressed) when we move towards something negative, ugly, hateful, repellent, frightening, painful, depressing. That takes us down on the energy chart.**

It really could not be any simpler than that.

It is practical, highly effective, works beautifully. It's also reliable, repeatable, testable - a real law of nature.

I sum this principle up by saying:

**"If you fill your mind to overflowing with beautiful things,
there can be no room left for doubt."**

Raising Energy

There are literally a myriad of different ways to raise energy.

Raising energy means to get out of stress, and into success. It's a good thing to be doing, all the time, every day, as often as possible.

I can raise my energy ...

- by looking up at the sky;
- by taking a deep breath;
- by giving my partner a loving touch (or receiving one);
- by stroking the cat;
- by having a delicious shower or a bath;
- by listening to music I love;
- by wearing special jewellery that serves as an anchor;
- by thinking about something sexy,
- by paying attention to beautiful things,
- by working on a project that inspires me,
- by touching base with inspiring people,
- by singing and dancing,
- by doing creative things ...

I can raise energy in all sorts of different ways.

How about you?

What do you do to raise energy that is natural, non-addictive, easy, and most of all, always works for you?

Take a moment to sit back and reflect on the many ways you already know how to raise energy when you need it.

The fact is that there are infinite opportunities all around, all the time, we could use to get ourselves higher - *we just didn't know how important it was, or where it would lead us.*

71

How To Make Friends (And Influence People)

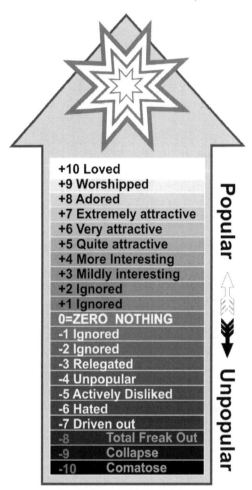

+10 Loved	
+9 Worshipped	
+8 Adored	Popular
+7 Extremely attractive	
+6 Very attractive	
+5 Quite attractive	
+4 More Interesting	
+3 Mildly interesting	
+2 Ignored	
+1 Ignored	
0=ZERO NOTHING	
-1 Ignored	
-2 Ignored	
-3 Relegated	
-4 Unpopular	
-5 Actively Disliked	Unpopular
-6 Hated	
-7 Driven out	
-8 Total Freak Out	
-9 Collapse	
-10 Comatose	

One of the fascinating side effects of higher energy states is the X-Factor, and "popularity."

Of course, the mysterious "je ne se quoi" or the so called X-Factor, that would be our neglected friend, the energy body.

You can look like a mutant from outer space on the outside, but if your energy body is firing on all cylinders, you'll be loved, adored, celebrated and everyone wants to be your friend.

In the converse, you can look like the most plastic perfect model from the outside, but if your energy body is a desperately screaming horror behind the scenes, you won't be finding love, only more pain.

And keep on wondering why ... oh why ...

People become more social, more socially powerful and more socially capable in a direct cause and effect fashion, the higher they rise on the energy chart.

The brighter the energy system, the more "attractive" it becomes to others who are seeking energy, who are hungry for energy, as everyone always is on the wrong side of the SUE scale.

Energy hungry folk will be drawn to a bright energy system like moths to the flame. Or if you want another way to describe it, an ordinary looking man might have "a lion heart," and other men will follow him to the ends of the earth.

Or we could say that it is a shiny, bright flaring energy system that makes a person "a star."

As I said, wherever you go and whatever you do, you get a great big, "AHA!" when you start to factor in the energy system.

Now, the question of "Why can't I find love?" is answered simply and profoundly, as well as the direct path to "What do I need to do to become more popular?"

Raise your energy ... it's easy ...

There is more to this than just becoming amazingly popular though.

On the right side of the SUE Scale, your star potential becomes revealed so you attract more love and attention from others. You also unlock a whole host of those mysterious "resources" that we've heard so much about but did not know how or where to find them.

Not only simple linear, mechanical intelligence, but also the far more complex, organic "Emotional Intelligence" starts to happen on the positive side of the SUE Scale.

So, we have all these new nerds who love to pride themselves on having no emotions, being ever so reasonable and rational, but people keep being out of reach to them, they don't understand how to conduct relationships, can't find friends, can't find lovers ...

You cling on to the Zero of Nothing, that's the thanks you get.

And worse, it's only down from there.

At Zero, you have Zero friends in your address book. You attract Zero sexual interest. Zero respect. Zero positive attention ...

Need I go on?

If you're one of those people who have been indoctrinated into the "no emotions is best" nonsense, don't beat up on your past aspects.

We were all taught the wrong things. It's a tragedy. But here we are, and now we can go forward.

Like any other normal human being (and my definition of "normal" certainly includes those who can buy a book, and then read it!), ___*you can go higher.*___

When you do, reality changes completely.

You gain access to more of your own, inborn intelligence, your own potential, your own mind, body and spirit.

And the higher you get, the more societal rewards await you.

Popularity is just the tip of the iceberg.

Leadership and respect also go to the people with the best energy system.

Now that's interesting, isn't it.

Turns out that it's not all about being more aggressive, being more scary, being more brutal than the next guy.

Turns out that with a strong and powerful energy system, with the "lion heart" at its centre, you get to be the leader.

Especially highly stressed people want to "follow" someone, anyone, who promises to lead them out of stress and into success will look to the leaders with the brightest energy systems.

Ah, and that explains the dictators ... and the blind followers as well ...

But now, back to the topic of this chapter.

How to win friends and influence people.

The answer is simple.

First, raise your own energy levels to at least +5 but hopefully above.

Now, you are "in energy profit" - that means you've something to contribute, something left to give.

You can now raise other people's energy levels.

This is now within your power.

You can literally inspire people (raising their spirits, raising their energy levels!)

You can make people glad that you are around, and you have it within your power to make people happy/er.

People like this.

They will love you for it.

But much more importantly, when you raise another person's energy levels, **they become better people,** so they will treat you better in return.

The same principle holds for other people as well - the more they have, the more they have to give to you.

That raises your energy levels even higher, automatically, without having to work hard at it.

This is a naturally upward lifting spiral.

Quite amazing, actually.

What we need to learn, understand and then, to enact, is to raise people's energy levels *unconditionally.*

Only Energy

Stress is "nothing" in and of itself; it is simply the absence of energy.

There is only energy,
and the absence of energy.

The dark side of the SUE Scale is "a poverty of energy."

Energy is like light in that way. A shadow doesn't have an existence, it is simply the absence of light. You cannot fight a shadow, and that's why "the war on stress" can't be won from that perspective.

- **Stress is the absence of energy; success is the presence of energy.**

The more energy, the more success. That's how it works.

We have observed that the more energy poverty exists, the more difficult/crazy/stupid people become.

They also become short sighted, deaf to reason, insensitive, egocentric, paranoid, amoral, driven by instant gratification. They steal, cheat, lie, and show us all the dark underbelly of humanity.

In the absence of even having the bright side of the SUE Scale to strive towards, we are left with the old style tit for tat approach: "If thine eye offends thee, cut it out."

Super stupid, super short sighted, a classic short sighted stress response, enshrined in law and religion everywhere.

You have to punish people who behave badly.

It just doesn't work. Ask the people who have to pay for keeping all these prisoners in prison in the USA, for example. It gets worse and worse, with no end in sight.

Stress your entire population hard and long enough, they go berserk on mass, and then we have riots, a revolution ... heads will roll ...

We're not talking about rapists, mass murderers, terrorists and other supermax security inmates here.

We are talking about every day people who work as call centre operators, policemen and women, fire fighters, taxi drivers, managers, secretaries, social workers, doctors, psychologists, scientists, teachers, bakers, bankers and candle stick makers, who are getting sick and ever more distressed because of stress.

The heart of the Trillion Dollar Stress Solution is that you need to seriously think about making people happier.

Happy beyond that awful place of nothing at Zero.

75

Happy beyond the "hippie fish tank" from -2 to +2, where people are drifting around aimlessly, "Yeah man ... chill man ..." style.

Happy to at least +3 but preferably +5, where the good things really start to happen.

We need to do this **unconditionally**, which means that happiness isn't dependent on how well a person performs, or how many hoops they can be made to jump through before eventually, finally, miraculously, something good happens to them.

It also means (heresy alert on!) that we must stop punishing people for doing wrong.

We need to re-set our entire mode of behaviour towards other people in order to make progress.

The ground rule is that to change anyone for the better, we need to give them more energy.

To change anyone for the better,
we need to give them more energy.

To get away from having to beat up the wife for cooking substandard, awful meals, we need to enact an order and sequence of events that will raise her energy so she becomes a better cook.

We may look for what we can praise - the fact she managed to get something on a plate without burning the house down, that's a start, "Well done, Daisy!"

We may offer positive, beneficial ways of learning more about food production - we might take her on a trip to a farm shop, or a restaurant, where she can have a good time and absorb more needed information.

We can love her, smile at her and make her performance *unconditional* on how we are treating her.

This will give her a space of freedom to breathe, to relax, to learn, to feel empowered, to make less mistakes, to perhaps even eventually evolve into a fine, creative cook.

Who is to say?

What we can say with certainty is that if we keep on beating up poor Daisy for her bad dinners, there is no hope for the future. There is only more and more suffering, more and more chaos, fractionation, atrophy and at the end, death of the relationship, death of any remaining potential that ever was.

- **It is a law of nature that by adding energy into any system, it becomes a better system. Add enough energy, and it will transcend, organise itself to a higher state, and that's really what we're looking for.**

In practice, we need to look at all the contexts in which stress plays a major factor, with fresh eyes and a whole new approach.

Instead of shaming and blaming endlessly, looking to the past all the time, punishing what's wrong in the sad hope that somehow something right will come of it somehow, we need to first of all, STOP.

It doesn't matter if you're dealing with yourself, your spouse, your head of department, your dog, your dolphin, your entire factory floor or the whole country if you're its leader.

The principles are always the same.

- **Raise people's energy, by any means you can think of to do so, and you will be dealing with better people.**

- **Lower people's energy, by any means you can think of, and you will always be dealing with worse people.**

To understand the logic and validity of this, unfortunately you have to be on the right side of the SUE Scale.

The vast majority of "leaders" today are on the wrong side. They are permanently stressed, permanently stuck on the wrong side of Zero.

And there, it's all about dog eat dog, and even the notion of "unconditional love," or "unconditional rewards" to create better people and a better world, seems totally alien, preposterous, our aforementioned heresy, in fact.

Yet THE FACT remains that at any time you engage that system of providing people with more energy, you will be blown away by the rewards it brings.

It has nothing but beneficial repercussions, and this becomes exponentially more noticeable, the more time passes.

Creating New Harmony Programs

After you have observed the effects on energy body stress on people in your environment (and on TV, in movies, in song and tale!) for a time, there naturally comes the time when you might want to take action.

For example, you might have a child, a boy of 9 years of age. You have become aware that he wakes up happy and plays happily, but then you tell him to get ready for school and the entire child changes.

He becomes angry, stroppy, non-co-operative. You start to argue, you start to fight. A long drawn out battle ensues to get the clothes on, find the shoes, find the homework, get the kid into his coat and out of the house and into the car. When the child is finally delivered at school, you sink into a state of exhaustion ...

Armed with the SUE Scale and the stress chart, and thinking in terms of aspects, we can begin to notice a cause and effect here.

The child wakes up happy - he's in a good energy state. The word "school" causes that happy energy state to collapse, creating the next aspect - the angry, stroppy, STRESSED, low energy version of the same child.

So after a month or so of observing this every single day, perhaps we can make some kind of change here ...?

Test the theory ...?

What could we try out ...?

The theory says that **we need to raise the energy to have a nicer child.**

His energy body collapsed on the word or thought of having to go to school ... Hmm ....[2]

But we're here. We've said the word, "School." The magic word that caused instant systems failure.

Now we could sit down on the bed, pat the side and say, "Hey, come, sit here for a moment."

The boy pouts, shuffles closer, sits down quite a way away.

"Daddy loves, you, do you know that?"

... ?

I wrote this example as it came to me.

All sorts of things could have happened next. The child may or may not have co-operated better after a moment of positive attention from his dad.

---

2 *If that was my child, I would certainly ask him why the very thought of having to go to school is causing an extreme and imminent energy body collapse. I would find out what scares him so, and do something about it. I certainly would not let this go on for any length of time and wait until the child begins to develop stress induced illnesses, allergies, learning disorders, mood disorders or self mutilatory behaviours. Most of all, I would make sure the child knows about energy body stress and knows methods he can use to help himself when I am not present to protect him in person.*

What I'm saying is that **the "old river of events" was broken on this occasion, and a space for something new to emerge was created.**

This is what energy awareness does for you.

It allows for new ideas, new approaches, for trying something different rather than sinking into exhausted depression and giving up.

"Giving up the ghost ..." That's a popular term for someone whose energy system has just left the building ...

I cannot know what your problems are with your own stress, or with the stressed people you have to be dealing with.

Once again, I call upon your natural intelligence, and the experience you have gathered with people over your entire lifetime so far, be it 12 years or 120, on this planet.

I am going to ask you to stop thinking of the people in your life as "old mum," "old Joe," "little Lucy" and start thinking in terms of aspects now.

You know exactly what "good old mum" can be like, and what "bad old mum" is, when that aspect comes into being.

You also know exactly what makes "old mum" happy/er and what is going to wind her up even worse and will predictably turn her into "nightmare mum."

If you take a moment to put your hands on your heart, breathe deeply, and raise your own energy levels, you will see that fighting with these people in the old way is a waste of time, an ancient, dusty, rotten labyrinth from which there is no escape, only death.

Breathe deeply, focus on something you love and raise your energy.

As your energy goes up, you become empowered.

You become powerful.

You have it within your power to make people happy/er - and thus, create better people for you to be dealing with.

There comes a point when everyone is together and empowered at the same time.

When that happens, relationships change completely.

Indeed, you could say, and I would say that, you don't even know what a relationship should be like until both parties are at a +5 *at least.*

That's where we get into sync, that's where we get into "Harmony" - that's where the Harmony Program got its name.

The old models, including the SUD Scale, the Yerkes-Dobson and the Hebbian model, stopped at Zero.

That's a sad, lonely place, a literal no-man's land where there is neither joy, nor sorrow.

It is a terrible place to be.

We come to life, come into our own, and discover who we and other people "really" are, as well as what we can actually accomplish when we work together, from +5 onwards.

That's the new goal.

That's the new direction.

It's not a fairy tale.

These high energy states and experiences are "out there."

We simply need to develop the desire to get to them.

We need to be inspired, and we need to be unleashed ...

The Law of Energy & Attention

Some time ago, I saw a black preacher man on a conservative white TV News channel, in an argument with the rather clever host, a typical white dominant male in a fabulous suit, with a fabulous watch, about 50 years of age ...

The black preacher man was going on about the poor, and how more needed to be done for the poor.

The white man in the fabulous suit leaned back in his chair, and then said, "We have already spent BILLIONS on the poor - and it's not getting any better! How much more do you want us to spend on them? What more do you want?"

And the preacher man stuttered and spluttered, and couldn't find an answer.

I was outraged.

As a preacher, a so-called "man of God," *he should have known the answer*.

The poor don't need even more money thrown at them to make them go away.

That's like throwing money at a child to make it go away - "Get out of here, I don't want to see you, I don't want to interact with you, go buy an ice cream, go to the cinema, I don't care, just get yourself away from me!"

What the poor need is that someone finally gives a damn.

They need someone to turn around, and instead of endlessly ignoring them and telling them to get lost and sort themselves out, for someone to PAY ATTENTION.

To GIVE ATTENTION.

To give ENERGY.

That's what the preacher should have said.

"We don't want more money. We want someone to care, someone to love us, to respect us, someone to inspire us, to help us not be so afraid, stressed, anxious all the time. To raise our energy levels so we have more to give to each other, to our children, to society - and to you, my friend in the fabulous suit!"

It's a lack of love that causes riots.

A lack of respect, a lack of care, a lack of compassion - however you want to call this particular tomato a tomato.

People riot when they get too energy deprived, too stressed.

And "the poor" are far more stressed than the general already thoroughly stressed population, because they have all the problems of the rich as well as not having any time off in wonderful locations, on their yachts, no fun and games with wonderful food and drink, money hungry bright young things throwing themselves into their paths, with fabulous suits and awesome watches.

"The poor" are living in energy sapping environments, don't get to have fun in nature, don't get respect from anyone, don't get positive attention from "the man" or anyone else, for that matter, and spend their lives being afraid of not being able to survive, and being afraid of each other.

This directly results in "worse people" and that's why you find poor people doing badly in life, poor people's kids doing badly at school, poor people in jail, poor people stealing, poor people lying, and poor people eventually rioting and wanting to cut the heads off anyone who has a fabulous suit, and a cool watch.

So watch it, my rich and powerful friends ... There are more of them than there are of you ...

On the bright side, if folk would only finally get their heads around the extreme importance of understanding our energy bodies, our energetic relationships, and the extreme effects this produces, we could save so much money.

All the billions spent on "the poor" could start to make a difference. We could think of different ways to spend this money.

We could make energy body stress relief the central core of our spending on "the poor."

And it would all start by finally paying attention, rather than to try and make the poor simply disappear.

A few thoughts on how energizing the poor would be of help, in any country of the world.

A more energized person is less likely to turn to drugs to try and blot out the misery of their existence. They are less likely to become pregnant for no good reason. Being energetically in profit, they have something to give and want to work - not only that, they are good citizens and good employees who want to contribute, learn, advance, make more of their lives. They are better parents, so the next generation will grow up happier and healthier, do better at school, be less likely to be inspired by becoming a gangster ...

The list goes on ... and the knock on effects go on and on and on, and on, and on, and on ...

So let's talk about health, for a moment.

And not just the endless problem of how to fund health care for all the poor ...

Stress, Energy & Health

As we have observed, the energy body transmits "how it feels" through the 6th Sense, the physical sensations that have no physical origin.

So, for example, when you're told, "YOU'RE FIRED!" it feels like a punch to the stomach, but there was no physical contact at all, just an energy form that was transmitted from the boss, to the now ex-employee who feels like they're going to throw up.

Of course, their head hurts so much, it feels like it's blowing apart as well, they can't think straight, and all the rest ...

The core message here is that *emotions are very, very physical*.

They're not in the head.

Emotions are in the body, and they create havoc in the physical body.

It is a travesty that to this day "medical science" has not found a connection between stress and heart attacks. Yes, really. Look it up on the internet if you don't believe me. It's preposterous, ridiculous, stupid, typical "modern science."

It's no wonder people are leaving off the worship of the "Gods in the white coats" in their droves.

Ladies and gentlemen, and all others, let me tell you this piece of thoroughly unscientific news.

Stress causes heart attacks.

It's a fact.

But stress "causes" a lot more than just heart attacks.

Stress - the energy body being chronically low on energy and struggling to keep going in spite of this dire state of being - weakens the entire totality[3].

Stress causes accidents, for example. The more stressed a person is, the more mistakes they will be making. You can check that for yourself; try typing a letter at speed when you are angry, nervous, or upset. You will make more spelling mistakes and typing errors than you would if you weren't so stressed. On a good day, or when you're "in the zone," there are no mistakes at all.

This is a global occurrence. Stressed drivers cause accidents; stressed people are far more likely to stumble and fall; stressed people are far more likely to fall off ladders, down stairs, trip over pavement cracks. Stressed people miss warning signs and important hazards as their attention skips and wanders from one thing to the other. If they're operating heavy machinery, they might lose limbs that way, run over fellow employees, shoot comrades by "accident" - all this gets worse and the incidences more frequent and more severe, the more stressed normal people become.

---

3   *I use the term "totality" for a whole human being, mind, body, spirit, all of it together as a single system.*

83

Just a ten percent reduction in work related accidents and injuries, and traffic related accidents and injuries, what would that amount to in the country you come from? Have a think ...

That's the tip of the iceberg, though.

Stress disturbs the entire totality of the human systems, and the higher the stress, the worse the repercussions are for the individuals concerned.

So, we have stressed executives, but also mothers, fathers, youngsters these days having heart attacks.

Older people might also have strokes, and these things are extremely expensive in every way you want to measure this.

There's more.

When the energy system becomes weak, the body becomes vulnerable to all manner of viruses, bacteria, pathogens, and even becomes hyper sensitive to perfectly normal things in the environment.

We have colds, flues, rashes, infections, allergies, and it's getting worse and worse.

That's stress. Of course, our science friends in their white coats will immediately jump up and say, "There's no evidence that stress makes the immune system weak and vulnerable at all ..." and of course, once again, I'll just shake my head in sorrow.

Instead of listening to some paid mouthpiece quack who is always trotted out by the big pharmaceutical companies and the powers that be when it comes to bashing anything remotely holistic, ask an old family doctor who's been looking after real people for fifty years. Ask one, ask a hundred, ask ten thousand. Find those old doctors in every country of the world, and they will all say the same thing - when people become stressed, all manner of illnesses start to manifest.

Whatever is already wrong with the person becomes worse, and can become critical if the stress is high enough.

It really doesn't matter what it is in each individual case that "flares up" when stress becomes higher, stress causes flare ups.

In eczema, in back pain, in migraines, in hay fever, in diabetes, in impotence. Which sends people running to the doctors in search of a cure ...

Now imagine just ten percent less "stress flare ups" would send ten percent less people running to the doctors in your country. What saving would that amount to for your creaking health system?

So this is just a quick fly over tour of stress and health.

A few side notes.

"Medical research" has never taken into consideration that you're not dealing with one person, but with at least 21 different aspects according to the stress chart.

These 21 different aspects will have totally different body chemistries, depending where they happen to be on the stress chart.

Likewise, they will react differently when you give them an aspirin, depending where they happen to be on the stress chart.

In theory, all medical research to date would have to be re-done, and one of the variables that needs to be controlled is the state of stress in the research subjects.

Indeed, one of the first things we would have to do is to take a good selection of people, and take snapshots of their respective body chemistry at each one of the 21 stages of the stress chart. You would have to learn how to put people into the exact state you want them to be in, naturally, and that you can't do without taking emotions and the energy body into consideration.

This would be the first step - to create a medical SUE Scale as a basic reference point. The next step would be to test people for these different states before declaring them to be suffering from (x, y and z).

By all means, don't forget to take the blood of people at +10. Study it very carefully - what's in THEIR blood that the stressed people at -5 don't have? Perhaps we can finally have a happy pill that really works? Find the cure for cancer? That would be nice ...

Strictly for physical health, and nothing else, to not pay attention to emotional stress, aka the state of the energy body, **is complete insanity.**

Still, it goes on, and still, we - you and me, and everyone we love! - are practically paying the price for the closed minded, stress induced stupidity of "the powers that be."

We are paying that price in money, every day, as we are being made to bail out failing health systems and having to pay ever more for our own health care; we pay this price in bad service, lack of attention, lack of love; we pay this price in even more emotional suffering as we and those we love become ever unhappier, become sick, suffer.

For nearly 20 years now, there has existed a super simple "stress relief" technique, EFT, I've already mentioned it, and for all that time, thousands of good people have been pulling their hair out because "We can't get EFT into ..." (schools, hospitals, prisons, etc.).

EFT has no side effects. It can be learned in 10 minutes by a five year old child. It needs no drugs, no qualifications to teach it, and it works first time out of the gate with 85% of people who try it.

But it's energy based. It doesn't sell more chemicals. It's heresy.

So let's ignore it and hope it'll go away ...

"If you think I'm going to re-write my manuals, you've got another thing coming ..."

Yeah ...

And in the meantime ...

Last week, my partner and I went to look at a motor home for sale. Without me saying a single thing about what I do, the man who was selling it started to tell me

85

about his wife, how she was suffering from anxiety, how it was getting worse, the side effects of the pills, how sad he was that he had to sell the motor home because she could no longer leave the house ... how he was now suffering from depression because of it ...

One tragedy out of ... how many million? Billion, even?

Could the woman's anxiety have been cured with EFT?

Who knows? Nobody tried! Nobody gave her the chance to have a go when she first went to the doctors with her first symptoms. 6 years ago, 14 years after EFT was available in principle to everyone at all who wanted it.

It's a tragedy, it's a travesty.

It makes me very angry - so please excuse me for a moment, dear reader, while I take a deep breath, imagine my hands on my heart in the Heart Position even as I type on, and find something to love.

There are many things that I love, but most of all, I love the fact that we have the Internet; that for the first time in human history, a person such as myself can't simply be silenced as my young aspect was back in day. Today, I have a way to address people - person to person, human being to human being, just as I am talking to you now.

This I love; and I love to have this opportunity.

I hope that I am making sense to you, and you will understand that I am a passionate person who's been banging her head against the wall of stress induced stupidity, greed and closed mindedness for over three decades now, for 33 long years as I write this.

It is incredibly annoying to have figured out something that would help so many, and not being able to bring it forward and make good use of it.

Well, hopefully with this book, the right people will find it, and perhaps there's a measure of hope that there are people out there who want to make more money, want to be happier, and want to make the world a better place who will eventually get to hear of this.

So!

Back to the story.

We had been talking about health, and how stress makes people sick.

That's the physical story.

Where it gets truly vertigo inducing is when we start to talk about "mental health."

No! You're Not Mad, You're Just Stressed!

I wanted to write a book with that title but couldn't find a publisher.

Not surprisingly ...

The medical profession can't really get their heads around "mental illness" unless there's a tumour or a bullet lodged in the brain.

The "mental specialists" in medicine, the psychiatrists, try to control behaviour and thinking with drugs. They deal with crazy people ...

But who is actually really crazy?

That's a good question.

I have met many, many people who had all and every "mental health" diagnosis under the sun - and it turns out they had just been very stressed at the time they went to see a doctor, and were duly diagnosed with (x, y and z).

The fact is that stress affects our emotions and our thinking far more radically than the body, which is relatively slow to respond and produce the symptoms. It takes a while before the constantly churning stomach created by stress at work turns into ulcers, before the thumping terrified heart starts to throw an epileptic fit.

Stress affects emotions, behaviour and thinking **instantly and immediately**.

As we've already discussed, when energy levels plummet fast, we can get from lovely wonderful husband Peter to road rage monster criminal Peter in under a second. That's fast - that's energy at work.

- **I think we need to seriously re-appraise our ideas of sanity and insanity in light of the stress chart and the SUE Scale.**

I would offer the following rule of thumb.

If you take a person out of a stressful environment and do the right things so their energy body restores and re-charges, and all the symptoms of "mental illness" disappear, they were never crazy at all - just highly stressed.

If you take a person out of the stressful environment, do all the right things, and they still scream about demons, then they're probably really mentally ill.

I would say that as it stands, there are many people who think they're crazy, and they're not crazy at all.

There are many people suffering needlessly from the symptoms of stress that get ever worse, the more stressed you become, who could be living perfectly happy, normal lives if only they knew about the Stress Chart.

There are many, many people right now who are on a downward stress spiral, who could halt that slide right now and turn it the other way - from stress to success, as I've coined it so it can be a popular phrase.

There are further, many people who have to deal with stressed people, at work, in their family, who could significantly help those stressed people turn the tide and start to feel better.

In the UK, it came to pass that a new government was elected on a ticket of austerity measures. Rather than going after giant businesses like Google who pay no tax at all, it was decided to go after the worst spongers and layabouts who don't contribute a thing to society - the disabled unemployed.

To this end, a private company was hired who was given targets. A percentage of people were to be knocked off the register altogether so they would receive no further payments at all; a percentage of people who would somehow be coaxed, coached and forced back into work (the private company was given lots of reward money for those!); and to reduce benefits as much as possible by moving as many as possible into different, cheaper categories where they would receive much less support for everyone else.

The sheer misery, anxiety, stress, unhappiness this caused amongst those people, many of whom were already in chronic pain, on crutches, in wheelchairs or bedridden, having cancer, life threatening diseases, dying, alone, penniless, old and generally, surely quite downtrodden enough, can't be overestimated.

I knew a number of people who suffered from this, suffered through this and are suffering still, and I thought, if only there would be some common sense here.

Giving each one of these disabled people an EFT protocol to try, for example, that would be one single sheet to print out that could have been included with the endless threatening/terrifying letters and incomprehensible questionnaires they were being bombarded with.

It would have made sense to the private company; for just one individual who may have alleviated their stress and anxiety enough, raised their energy levels enough to say, "Yes, OK, I think I can now handle re-training as a computer support person, working from home ..." would have brought that company huge, huge profits.

Just one single success in that whole million would have paid for all those leaflets ...

This is just one of the daily examples where I see how modern stress management techniques, energy body centred stress management techniques, and in the end, HEART CENTRED stress management techniques could have helped, could have made a difference.

Alleviated suffering.

Stopped further stress declines into even worse physical and mental health.

Saved lots of money.

MADE LOTS OF MONEY.

There is no downside for individuals, no downside for societies in at least giving simple methods like EFT or EMO a chance.

There is no reason whatsoever to not at least try this out.

The only reasons for trying to keep modern energy techniques out of the mainstream are the vested interests by those who don't want to update their training manuals, and of course, our old friends, the pharmaceutical companies which have their tentacles everywhere and will try to extinguish anything that isn't making vast profits for them, with their pet universities, armies of paid "scientists" and paid politicians in their pockets ...

This is sadly, a fact; but I am calling for a ground roots revolution here.

So you're a manager and you can't be seen to be tapping EFT, and it's not your job to teach those under you about the stress chart even though this would transform the effectivity of your section, make the workplace a better place to be and give you the strength and power you need to do a sterling job, day, in, day out.

So you're a social worker, and you are not allowed to tell the terribly stressed people you have to deal with every day, including your colleagues and your clients, about energy bodies, emotions and modern stress management.

So you're a nurse, or a doctor, and you can't be seen to be tapping EFT for your own stress, or teach your patients to tap so they heal faster and get out of that precious hospital bed sooner.

So you're a teacher, and you can't be seen to teach the kiddies in your class a bit of EMO to help them totally transform their lives, lose their social fears, their blocks to learning reading and writing and maths, their test terrors, their temper tantrums.

- ***You can still use your own creativity and your own intelligence to raise your own energy first of all in every way you can.***

You can't be fired for stopping for a moment, placing your own hands on your heart and taking a deep breath, in and out.

You can't be fired for having a picture of your lover, your child or your cat hidden in your locker, and use that on breaks consciously and deliberately to bring your energy levels up.

You can't be fired for "thinking energy" and finding creative ways to bring energy levels up in other people, a smile, a bit of attention, a loving approach that comes from your true heart.

Thank God for that.

In the meantime, I keep hoping and praying that the day will finally come, that sanity will somewhere finally prevail, so that our manager, our teacher, our nurse can openly help people, openly talk about energy AND EMOTIONS, openly encourage other people to learn to read their own stress levels right, and those of other people, and discuss further ways in which we can get energy levels to be HIGHER.

That's the goal.

"You know that it would be untrue ...
"You know that I would be a liar ...
"If I was to say to you ...
"Girl, we couldn't get much higher ..."
Jim Morrisson

HIGHER

People under stress yearn for peace.

No longer feeling all those burdens dragging you down, the heavy gravity, the fear that never ever leaves you ...

(I read somewhere that by the time a human is over 40, they have more stress hormones in their systems when they are asleep than a zebra that's just been chased by a lion.)

(Stressed people can't sleep properly, did you know that? Their dreams aren't right either. And without sleeping right, the next day becomes even harder ... and go on like that for a few years, what state will you be in when you're 45, 50 ...?)

The more you yearn for some form of peace, of not having to worry any more, to just being able to relax and breathe deeply, in freedom, letting it all go ...

... the more stressed you are.

I do have to tell you this though.

- **Peace is a very dangerous thing.**

It's what I call "a death goal."

When we offer up the idea of lying flat on your back, with a beatific smile on your face, and never having to move ever again to our totality (mind + body + spirit, the whole "human package"), it goes on strike.

"I don't want to be dead - I want to be alive!"

Every part of our totality is life-driven.

None of it wants to be dead, ever,

This goes for every cell in your physical body, every nerve fibre, every organ, everything.

It also goes for your energy body. It doesn't want to be dead either.

"Death goals" - and peace is exactly that, that's why it says "R.I.P" aka "Rest in Peace" on headstones - are a road block to happiness.

- **Happiness lies on the other side of Zero.**

In fact, stressed people have made whole religions out of that.

"You live and suffer your whole life long, and it's only after death you get to experience joy, love and ecstasy, and that's how it's supposed to be."

The Zero point of nothing is no goal. Nothing is a no go as far as inspirational goals are concerned.

I can't tell you just how important it is to set our sights HIGHER.

Much, much, much HIGHER.

If you haven't really experienced the joy of the real high energy states in your life yet, you might not quite appreciate what I'm talking about here.

At +10, you are completely transformed.

90

You are a different person, literally.

Your body chemistry is completely different in every way.

You are what I like to call "the other."

A few things I would like you to know about these high energy states.

1. They are your birthright - God (or the structure of the Creative Order) made you the way it made you, and it gave you the ability to experience "life at +10." That's a simple fact, and don't let any stress riddled religious zealot try and tell you any other.

2. The really high energy states don't last that long, although when you're in them, it appears that way, because time ceases to exist altogether. In clock time, you'll be in a +10 state for half an hour at the most, probably more like a couple of minutes, and the rest is afterglow.

3. It is very unlikely that you will get up and leave all your loved ones behind, to walk the earth with a begging bowl or any such nonsense. Propaganda of the ages has made the high energy states seem crazy and unattractive - when they are nothing of that sort.

4. The whole idea of the stress chart is not to get stuck anywhere, not even at +10. Moving smoothly up and down the stress chart at will is what I would call ***emotional mastery***.

5. You don't know who you "really" are until you've met your +10 aspects. If you haven't experienced being one of those, you are most likely working from a faulty, badly skewed map and that's not reasonable/logical/practical.

What I have found is that the lower people are on the stress chart, the more afraid/anxious/stressed they are, the more the idea of the +10 terrifies them.

It seems like a crazy, alien concept at -7; at -4 (where most of the population spends most of their time), it seems that it's not safe, and it's better to "stay with what we know."

-4s cling to the old like a terrified drowning victim clinging to a piece of flotsam; or in the way a terrified person clings to the rung of a ladder and simply can't let go. That's where being "conservative" ("We are so low on energy, we must CONSERVE every little bit or else all is lost!") comes from, and it's just a classic fear response, and that's all it is.

In the no man's land around Zero, -2 to +2, there is no reason to do anything at all. A lot of middle class and lower middle class as well as upper working class people hover permanently around this level, living the American dream, filling their lives with pointless consumerism, watching TV and basically just drifting along aimlessly from one day to the next, unless there's a tragedy of some kind, or a comedy, that will snap them out of it for a short time.

It's only from +3 and above that folk finally start looking up, seeing the sky, smelling the roses, flexing their fingertips and saying, "Mmmh ... I can feel even better than this? I can be even more successful? That's starting to sound like a good idea now ..."

91

The rise up to the higher levels of the SUE scale isn't a linear rise. It is exponential.

From +3 to +5 is a huge leap, and from +5 to +7 an even bigger one. +8, +9 and +10 literally blow your mind, so we'll leave these for now.

What is important to understand, however, is that your spheres of influence increase or decrease with the rise and fall of your own energy body.

Your energy body is your personal power, not your physical body.

The more functional, the stronger your energy body becomes, the more personal power you have and the more power you have to "change the world."

The converse is true as well - you can observe this in action in any hospice in the world.

The Dying Process

A hospice nurse once remarked on what they called "The Dying Process" that it seemed as though the dying patients were collapsing in on themselves.

Of course, that's the energy system collapsing in on itself, like a fire burning low, until there is only a small ember left. When this last ember becomes extinguished, the end has come.

The hospice nurse didn't know about energy bodies, but they reported how they had noticed that the "spheres of influence" were becoming ever smaller, in ever decreasing circles.

At first, the patients would still be interested in the news, what was going on in the world. Then they stopped being interested in that, but might still be aware of/interested in their favourite things, their football team, their family.

As this structural collapse of the energy system continues, they would only be interested in their family, and then, one particular person only. There would be one final flare up as they struggled against death, but in the end, they would not know anyone apart from themselves, and then that went away as well and they would die.

This is what happens on the stress chart to living people as they get lower and lower on energy, as their fire burns less and less brightly, flares up one more time, and then burns out.

The spheres of influence contract - the energy body contracts, like a retreating army making their final stand in the heart of their territory.

The connection with the world around them is lost in the process, and this gives us so many explanations for so many phenomena that occur to normal people as they shift into different states of being along the stress chart.

The lower you are, the more selfish you become. This is not because you become evil in some way, but simply because as the spheres of influence collapse around you, more and more other people are excluded and "cease to exist" - just like the dying process.

There can be no rapport, no compassion, no understanding or care for other people when *there are no other people any longer.*

The super-stressed "schizophrenics" talk about collapsing into themselves, into a tiny point of light; that's the dying process in action.

That's the energy body dying ... even when the physical body still seems to be perfectly healthy.

The stress collapse into the smaller and smaller spheres of influence is highly structural and observable everywhere; even entire societies and countries do this, for example, when in war all the lovely people who were so clear about the rights of humanity begin to exclude the enemy, and then those who collaborate with the enemy.

"The enemy" becomes structurally excluded from their sphere of influence under stress, and the higher the stress goes, the more people become excluded.

These "excluded people" can now be murdered at will without blinking an eye or having any moral problems with this, can be tortured, detained, stripped of all and every human right.

It's easy.

That's how you do it.

That's how you turn a peace loving hippie community into club wielding barbarians who turn upon their neighbour and each other.

Stress them to below -5.

"All the world is mad but me and thee,
and I think I have doubts about thee ..."

Beyond The Death Goals

We have already met the "Death Goals" - goals that happen naturally when people are terribly stressed and in emotional pain, all they want is for everything to STOP.

"I want to feel nothing ..."

In order to work with the energy system correctly, we need goals that inspire.

Visionary goals from the high energy states that have the power to uplift our energy systems in the very act of considering them.

If you start paying attention to the goals, hopes and dreams people have, it is shocking how that barrier at Zero holds people trapped on the negative side of the stress chart.

Consider your own goals.

Watch for goals that are set way too low, and most importantly, are based on some kind of inactivity or absence of activity.

Watch out for goals that once they have been reached, end with "... and they lived happily ever after ..."

There is no such thing as "... living happily ever after ..." until you're dead.

Before you're dead, there's LIFE happening - brutal, wild, exciting, amazing, challenging, beautiful, extraordinary.

I often use a little game with people beset by a death goal.

Let's take the "lying flat on your back on a tropical beach and never having to raise a finger again" fantasy, which is pretty much what a corpse under a palm tree would be.

Let's move on time.

"So you've lain there for a century, for a millennium. Are you bored yet? What happens next?"

Well, eventually they'll get up. And start looking around at what else there is. Who knows, they might take a walk on the beach, enjoy the cool evening breeze and the sweet water caressing their toes in the soft white sand ...

Now we're coming to life, just about ...

Perhaps they'll be ready to jump into the water, and swim for a while.

But even that, fun as it is, gets lonely.

Perhaps there'll be other people somewhere ...

We are slowly climbing up the SUE Scale, slowly reversing the death spiral, turning it the other way - outward and outward, embracing more and more, becoming more empowered along the way.

Eventually, we might be reaching a point where we are so HIGH, we're not searching out other people in order to be helped by them, satisfied by them in some way, but with the intention to help them, to satisfy them.

When that point is reached, popularity becomes near enough guaranteed, for a one who has something left to give to others is a rare treasure in this day and age of the global stress pandemic.

A one who has left something over at the end of a long day working and taking care of their family to give to the community at large is an asset to every community.

Now, wouldn't it behove the community to make it so that there would be more of those amongst us?

Indeed, what might a community where almost everyone has something to give be able to accomplish?

A global community, at that ...?

I leave that thought with you.

The 16.7% Advantage

The Trillion Dollar Stress Solution is to factor in the fact that humans really have an energy body.

This increases the incoming information into any human being by 16.7%*[4]

Instead of working with the evidence we can gather through five senses, we are working with six.

This doesn't seem a lot at first glance, but it's right inside that 16.7% additional knowledge where the lines are to be found which connect the dots of human thinking, doing and being.

Let's consider some questions that have haunted people for at least 2,000 years.

What's wrong with people?

They are too stressed. If they were happier, they would be smarter, nicer and generally, a real bonus to the Universe at large.

What's wrong with me?

Check with your "worst" aspects. How stressed were they? Chances are, what's wrong with you is that you too suffer from deep, ongoing stress that is much worse than you ever thought. Your energy body is a screaming mess, and it needs some attention, urgently. Then you'll feel better. Including about yourself.

Who am I?

You are a malfunctioning version of your "true self" most of the time. You are you and get to know who you are at +10.

Where can I find myself?

You find yourself at +10.

Why do so many people believe in magic and religion?

Because there is a real reality of invisible stuff going on all the time, and it's perfectly real, and magic and religion have tried to describe that and work with that. People can't live without trying to figure out what is going on with their non-material experiences. Simple.

What is the X-Factor?

It's the human energy body. You can't see it but you sure as hell can SENSE it. The higher the X-Factor, the more shiny the energy body. A very shiny energy body is super attractive and such people become "a star."

What is the missing link between inoculations and autism?

The energy body. Something bad happens in the energy body when massive amounts of viruses (who also have "energy bodies!) are injected into it all at the same time. This causes the energy system to collapse which produces "the symptoms of autism." What are the most obvious signs of autism?

---

4   *It's actually 16.666~ % but I've rounded it up! :-)*

Emotional instability and the inability to "connect" with other people. Truly, it couldn't be more straightforward if you tried.

What is the missing link between stress, and people having heart attacks and strokes?

The energy body. Duh.

How does Placebo work?

The problem wasn't in the physical body, it was in the energy body. The placebo created the opportunity for a change in the energy body - and the symptoms went away.

What is "the unconscious mind"?

The energy body has a heart of energy, and veins, they're called meridians. It has "healing hands" (hands that can touch other people's energy bodies and affect changes there) and it has a head. I call it the "energy mind." So and in brief - the unconscious or subconscious mind is actually the energy mind, or "the head of the energy body."

What is "the soul"?

The soul is a real energy system which exists in the energy body, but it has no reflection in any physical organ. So there is the structural possibility that when the body dies, and the energy body fades away, the soul can survive. And carry data from one life into another, should there be another.

How does poverty breed crime?

The lower on the energy chart you are, the more extreme the behaviours become. Poor people are more stressed than people who don't have to worry about where to get the next meal from, so they behave worse. Make rich people poor, and they too will become "criminals."

How do I get more sex out of my wife more often?

Check her stress levels. Alleviate her stress and move her up into the higher reaches of the SUE Scale. Around +5, she will come to life and when that happens, she will become very interested in sexual/sensual activities.

How do I get to be more popular/more attractive/luckier/richer?

Raise your energy body stress levels until you're at least a +5. That's where confidence and attractiveness begins.

Why does nobody love me?

Because you're too low on the energy scale, and all the other people are way too stressed to be wanting an energy sucker near them, to bring them even further down. Get up on the SUE scale so you start to shine and then people will cluster around you like moths around a flame.

NB. You just asking that tells me you're down in the dumps, as far as energy is concerned. Raise your energy levels!

By the time you get to +3 you start remembering that there are people who love you now or have loved you in the past ...

How can I save 3 1/2 million dollars of the money that stress costs my business every year?

Teach your staff Modern Stress Management. Hand them SUE Scales and SUE Wristbands. Work out what makes for "happier workers" and implement small changes designed to raise energy. Then sit back in astonishment at the results.

Why do high school students shoot up schools?

Doh! Because they weren't very happy. And nobody took notice of this, nobody paid attention to the energy problems at that school. That's the sort of difference our little 16.7% makes in the real world.

Why do people take drugs? And stay addicted to drugs?

*Because they are so unhappy, so miserable, in such long and ongoing energy body stress and depletion, they will do **anything** to feel better for a short period of time. And they stay addicted not only because of physical addiction, but because they don't want to let go of the only thing that's ever helped them, reliably. (This tells you something about the "rich kids" as well as the poor ones ...)*

Why do rock stars kill themselves?

They write songs in states of high energy body stress - and then re-evoke those high stress states every single time they perform their sad/angry/heart rending songs. It's very unhealthy. A real energy body killer in the long run.

Why do people buy energy drinks?

Because they know they're low on energy and try and find ways to get higher. Desperately.

Why does child sex abuse cause such tremendous repercussions?

The sexual circuitry in the energy body is the "main power conduit" for the energy body. You mess with that, and the entire energy body goes haywire. This gets worse and worse, the longer it goes on and remains untreated. It's basically like trying to live with an open sore smack in the middle of your body. Eventually, it takes over your entire life. The younger the child, the worse the repercussions. To the point that people will eventually die of this.

Why do people watch Oprah?

Because it gives them HOPE. That's an energy body state. It is de-stressing. It raises their energy levels. It HELPS people be a little bit smarter, stronger, faster and more loving than they were before the show started. That is the same principle upon which evangelism rests, and much more besides.

I could go on forever and ever with this, but that's not the point here.

The point is for you to start factoring in that missing 16.7% in your daily life, and apply it to the questions that make you scratch your head.

You will find, time and time again, that the 16.7% connect the dots and now, everything makes perfect sense.

It is veritably spooky to me that I'm the one who has to point this out.

But there we have it.

I've shown this to a lot of people, and I'm not saying that my theory is the answer to everything, but it's certainly a step in the right direction.

A much better model that fits reality much, much better.

There's hope for all ...

Even for religious fundamentalists.

We just need to get beyond the words, and into the meanings.

Words, Meanings & Energy

I was in a bar in Southern Pennsylvania, having a drink, when this guy comes and sits next to me.

He introduces himself as the minister of the local church, and tells me that God told him to come to the bar, and therefore, our meeting must be pre-ordained.

I chortle into my brandy and coke. Does that line really work for him, most of the time?

But I like playing with a good old hellfire preacher. They're fun.

So I don't tell him that I'm a modern energist, or that energy magic is one of my specialities. Instead, I ask him what the biggest problem and source of concern in his congregation may be.

"Sins of the flesh!" he cries immediately, "Sins of the flesh, that's the worst problem! Oh, if only we could overcome the sins of the flesh!"

I nodded seriously for I could tell that he was very serious about this, and asked the EMO question - "Where do you feel those sins of the flesh in your body? Show me with your hands!"

He immediately clasped both hands to just above his genitals.

"Oh it burns," he cries, "Oh! It burns!"

"Ah," I say, and note in passing that a couple of truck drivers have sidled in to partake of this interaction, "You need the love of Jesus to heal that! The love of Jesus is a bright white light, you know it well, it comes from above, just let it in, let it heal that place where the sins of the flesh reside!"

And the minister starts trembling and sweating, twitching, opens his arms and shouts, "I can feel it! Oh dear lord, yes, bring your healing to me!"

Then he jumped off the bar stool and started dancing around the room in joy. "The pain, it's gone! I've been healed! Jesus has healed me! Praise be the Lord!!!"

When he had recovered himself somewhat, he said, "This is amazing! Why did I never think to do this! It's so obvious - the healing light of Jesus! The sins of the flesh will be no more! My entire congregation will be saved!"

Then he offered to marry me, but luckily, my partner turned up just at that point and all was well with the worlds ...

To people who haven't a clue about energy bodies, or the actual, experienced REALITY of energy bodies in people's real lives, this seems - insane, deluded, weird, scary, bad, and wrong.

To people who have gotten their heads around the fact that energy bodies are quite real, we have a different reading of the same situation.

The man had a significant injury in his energy body, which he could feel all the time, as a burning pain. That's not in his mind, he's not crazy, it's in his body for real - that's the 6th sense, screaming at psychosomatic pain levels. It doesn't get much worse than that, the next step will probably be cancer, right there in that place where he feels the burning pain, in a few more years or months down the line.

As a Christian, he had already some experience in working with energy, and the "bright light of Jesus" is actually real energy that exists in the "oceans of energy" that we're a part of.

All I had to do was to make that CONNECTION between his injured energy body, and that which could heal it - and bingo.

Job done.

The moral of the story is this.

Once you factor in our seemingly small 16.7%, all sorts of things start to make sense that couldn't possibly make sense before.

Not only that, you can get through the words down to their actual meanings.

When that happens, I can simply call in the bright light of Jesus healing for a Christian who speaks those words and thinks in terms of these concepts - without having to argue doctrine first, or de-program the man first, or putting him into psychotherapy first.

And without having to convert to Christianity first.

It all simply makes perfect sense when you add energy into the equation.

Even the words that people say to you.

Words Of Energy

- *He is doing my (energy) head in.*
- *She broke my (energy) heart.*
- *She's a pain in the (energy) neck. Or (energy) ass ...*
- *I am under so much (invisible, energetic, yet entirely real) pressure.*
- *I feel like there's a wall (of energy) between us.*
- *I felt like I had been punched in the (energy) stomach when she said she wanted a divorce.*
- *I don't like the energy in this room.*
- *That guy sucks the life (the energy) right out of me.*
- *My (energy) knees went weak when he proposed to me.*
- *I'm going to wash that man right out of my hair ...*

Here's the deal.

People think people are completely unpredictable.

Completely crazy.

Totally incalculable in their various insanities and weirdnesses.

But nothing could be further from the truth.

Calculate in that missing 16.7% - and everything makes sense.

Well, almost everything.

I'm still searching for that which doesn't ...

Let Robots Be Judges ...?

Did you know that entire families, entire cities, entire societies can go up and down the SUE Scale as well?

Like the entity that is New York, before and after 9/11.

Where were they before the trauma, and where were they after?

You've got to be so, so careful with stressed entities.

They make terrible decisions, just like stressed individuals do.

The more stressed they are, the worse, the more stupid, the more short sighted and the more inhumane the decisions become.

In the past, and because people do know that under stress, awful decision come into being, people once more concluded that the only way to perfect law and order is to make laws from a state of having no emotions at all - the Zero State of Nothingness.

Let robots be judges ...

But that's the thing with the energy inclusive paradigm.

We know that Zero isn't the answer.

The decisions you take there, the laws you make, the solutions you come up with (for yourself, for your family, for your town, for your country, for humanity) are NEITHER GOOD NOR BAD.

That's not good enough!

- **GOOD decisions demand a GOOD energy state - +5 or above.**

GOOD decisions produce GOOD outcomes.

Not Zero decisions.

Further, Zero decisions have Zero energy in them.

They are totally uninspiring.

They do not have the power to stand up to the screaming of the highly stressed ones in emergency mode.

To be able not just to stand up to highly stressed individuals, combining into huge group bubbles that become highly stressed entities, you need +5 and above.

In other words, instead of totally unemotional judges, you need HIGH judges - people who are firing on all cylinders, are IN LOVE with people, the world, the universe around them, and who make amazing, creative, powerful, decisions and create enriching, energizing, and hugely powerful laws.

"I have a dream ..."

Yes, and you may recognise the quote, and the man, and the state that man was in when he gave the speech. The more sensitive ones amongst you may experience a little shiver or some other 6th sense reaction when you thought about that speech.

High energy people are the ones that really do have the power to change the world.

Not the bean counters, no matter how long and hard they may squawk and hide behind their fake authority, based on such things as "The Yerkes Dobson LAW of Arousal," 1908.

That is the same in art, as it is in science. That's the same in religion as it is in politics. That's the same in society and culture, as it is in business and economy.

Here's the rub.

All those bean counters could rise above that too, get on the right side of the SUE scale, and then they won't be pointless bean counters either any longer, but instead, human beings on that extraordinary journey of discovery to "Who am I?"

"You want to know who you really are? Easy.

"You are you at +10."

Energetic Relationships - Meet The Bubbles!

The very term "relationships" can strike terror in the heart of men and women alike, and it all seems so incredibly inexplicable, so incredibly complicated.

Add in the energy realities, and it all makes sense.

We have energy bodies, and those energy bodies can link up, combine, and form what I've termed a "couple bubble."

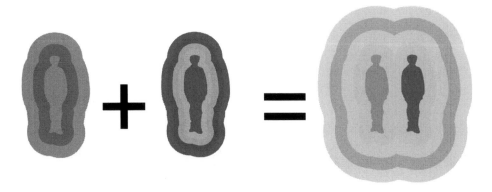

In this couple bubble, information is exchanged and the parties involved become more than the sum of their parts.

This can happen very rapidly, such as in "love at first sight," or it can develop over time, such as in a long drawn out Jane Austen type relationship that gets deeper and more profound slowly over time.

We can couple bubble not just with members of our own species, but also with companion animals, and there are some people who even couple bubble with objects.

Objects have an energetic existence too and so a fighter pilot can get to feel "at one" with his plane; a racing driver can feel "as one" with his car, and a good rider will feel "as one" with his horse - becoming more than the sum of the separate parts in the process.

- **A couple bubble is a whole new entity in its own right.**

To people who had previous energetic relationships with a single person, this can be very disturbing and cause grief and jealousy, further disrupting the old relationships (this is known as the Yoko effect).

The higher a person is on the SUE scale, the easier it becomes to couple bubble with everyone and everything. At the highest reaches, in the +10s, people always talk about "being one with God and all creation" - reliably so.

In our energy blind societies, it is taken for granted that if you have physical sex with someone that this means you have a strong "bond" - that you are couple bubbled to the greatest possible extent.

This is not necessarily the case.

Couple bubbles with brothers, friends and the aforementioned air plane, car and horse may be far more intense for a member of the "married couple" than the one they have with each other.

This is particularly so when one or both partners find interactions with other people intensely stressful, and are under high stress themselves.

- **To improve any relationship, you have to raise the energy levels in at least one of the members of the bubble.**

As always, it goes further.

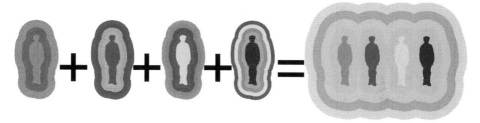

We can have group bubbles of families, sub-sets of families; in teams at work; social groups in schools, football team supporters, national identity bubbles, all sorts of energetic relationships that connect us with other people and the world.

The first step to improving any bubble, any relationship, is take a moment and ascertain how much stress there is in the bubble.

You can measure this by how well the bubble functions and how happy the individuals are within it.

- **A group bubble of highly energized individuals becomes a powerful "Mastermind" "group" with inordinate power to make things happen in the real world.**

A group bubble of highly stressed individuals will create chaos and more chaos, for themselves and for everyone who has to deal with them. When stress becomes too high, the bubble collapses altogether into smaller subsets, or totally disconnected individuals.

A good example of group bubbles are modern music groups and bands.

The more powerful the bubble, the more harmony there is between them, and the more amazing and powerful their music becomes. A band that is more than the sum of their parts attracts followers and has a better than average chance of success.

107

Often, what happens next is that stress sets in, the bubble bursts, as it were, leaving stressed individuals who are trying to make it work but it can't, which causes more stress, and then the band is dissolved.

What is important in MODERN Stress Management is that we don't look at an individual in isolation.

This is also one of the fundamental delineators between modern energism and the ancient oriental systems of energy work, which always featured a single individual (man!) sitting in the lotus position, with their "chakras" stacked up like dinner plates, one on top of the other.

Modern energism is about energetic relationships.

My bubble model is about energetic relationships.

If we remember back, my original studies were about social mammals, and the energy exchanges that happen *between* them.

This creates an organic, fluid model that can handle the complexities of reality quite simply.

No man is an island.

- **People are not designed to live alone.**

People have evolved to where they are and have not died out because they work together, because they form a group bubble, a tribe that is more than the sum of its parts.

All the bizarre ideas that permeate human philosophy and religions about linear hierarchies, men being better than women, old people being useless and children nothing but a burden and right down at the bottom of the heap, are based on severely stressed members of malfunctioning, dissonant, stressed groups.

When you actually have very highly energized individuals, something remarkable happens.

A group bubble comes into being that owns the experience of the old; just as it owns the power of the strong, and the curiosity of the young.

To be a part of a fully functioning, resonant group bubble is the most wonderful experience. It's in our DNA, it is how we're designed to be and it is hugely desirable.

It is this innate drive to bubbling with others of our species that has been perverted into strange religions and all manner of other strange things - yet it never goes away.

It is my assertion that we don't begin to function at the level that we could function as individuals unless we have the powerful support of a group bubble to lift us and makes us more than we could ever be by our lonesome selves.

That is a whole new level in the game of life, waiting to be unlocked, as modern individuals struggle with their personal development, take the next self improvement course.

If you want to truly change the world, you don't do it by yourself.

You need to bubble with high energy individuals who become the wind beneath your wings.

Now this may sound like fantasy fiction to you and to me.

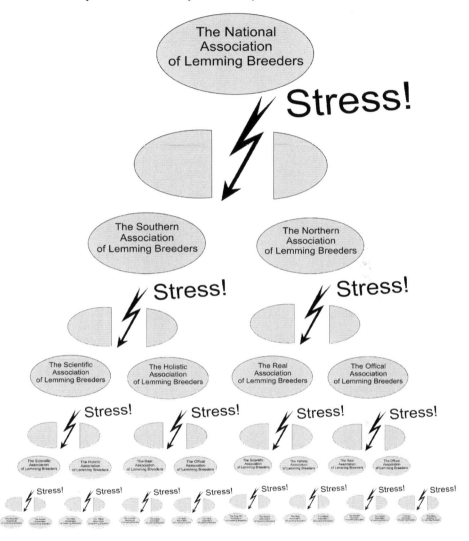

When we look at the living reality of our various bubbles, there is so little concordance, so little harmony, even within the ever fractionating "mini groups" as large bubbles break up into smaller, warring factions, and those break up, and those break up as well as stress gets higher and higher and energy levels, intelligence, effectiveness, sanity becomes ever less and less ...

You need energy to form strong, powerful bubbles.

To bring people together, be this in a partnership, a family, a band, a team, a block, a city, a country, you need to energize people.

Then they start to come into harmony, they start to stick together and get positive things done for themselves, and for each other.

The good news is that one single person can turn the tide.

In any group bubble, a single person who becomes more energized can help others become more energized too.

They have a surplus of energy - "The more you have, the more you have to give!" - and can start to energize other members of the group.

It's like a ripple in a pond.

As other people become more energized, the group bubble begins to stabilise and as soon as we get to even +3, we're coming onto the same page and start to look at our similarities, instead of our differences.

This is, once more, highly structural and works all the way from one man and his dog to the United Nations and every level in between.

Once more, it starts with a single person who understands how this works, raises their own energy into the positive reaches and by doing so, assumes a whole new type of leadership position.

Teaching & Learning

In 2014, I completely re-wrote the Trainer's Training for The Guild of Energists.

We teach people about modern energism, and we do this by providing them with experiences so they can test our assertions for themselves, and draw their own conclusions.

There is core material that has to be learned, such as our SUE Scale and Stress Chart, and how we work with that when we deal with stressed out clients, for example.

There is quite a bit of information, but the trainings are usually about giving people a chance to de-program and re-organise the experiences of their own lives in a new way.

Now, we had inherited a trainings model from the general way trainings are conducted - you get a room with people sitting on chairs, handouts manual on their knees, looking at the teacher who is standing in front of some white board or powerpoint presentation.

That's how people think about learning something without energy in mind. It's the ancient school/university model.

But that's not an optimal learning environment - if you factor people's energy bodies into the equation.

The most important difference energy awareness in learning makes is that a person absorbs exponentially more information in any environment, including a classroom situation, the more energized they are. We can sum that up by saying:

- **The higher you are, the more you learn.**

At -4, the state you would find the depressed and bored students in classes and lectures the world over (unless they're in some crazy religious fundamentalist school where they are constantly terrified to be beaten with sticks, in which case the students there would be closer to -7!) only very few disconnected data items can be absorbed.

At +4, students begin to actively absorb information, which also includes information about the teacher, about the other students in the class, and they will begin to make connections between the material presented in class and other information from elsewhere.

Get the students high enough, and the "data transfer" from the teacher becomes near enough instantaneous. The teacher has only to say something once, and not only is this information immediately "absorbed," it is sorted correctly and can be re-called at any time, permanently, unless severe stress interferes under special circumstances.

But that's not all.

There is more to it than that.

111

The higher people are, the more sociable they become.

Their energy systems combine and they form the "group bubble" where each person is more than the sum of their parts.

In the past, for example in the old religions, what happened was that the priest was trained how to do that - get everyone to sing together, breathe together, think together, and steer it from the front.

In modern energism, we've found a different way.

Namely, to raise the energy of the group to create the bubble - and then for the trainer to step inside of it as well.

Instead of disempowering individuals so they get "lost in the group," when you work with high energy individuals, you create the mystical "Mastermind" effect, as we have already observed.

When that happens, all the individuals start to also learn through and from each other and everyone ends up with tremendous gains.

We further observed this in action.

- **By working simply with the energy of the group and the individuals within the group, it becomes easy and natural to lead a group.**

It becomes easy and natural to teach people new things, and more importantly, for the teacher/trainer to LEARN from every group they lead, so they evolve as well.

In the old models, the teacher remained endlessly the same, like a rock in a stream, with the students flowing by like water.

No wonder it was such a drag to try and make connections with these teachers, why they failed to inspire us, why it was so hard to actually truly learn from them!

No wonder all forms of schooling is still such a drag - unless you are lucky enough to encounter that super rare individual teacher who has figured out how it works, and who can inspire their pupils, relate to them and *change with them when they change*.

The difference factoring in the energy of individuals, and that of the group, makes to teaching and training is breathtaking.

What's even more astonishing is how easy this is to affect.

All you need to have for this dynamic to start its upward spiral into success is for the person at the front to be high.

To be high on the SUE Scale instead of stressed, blocked up, unhappy and incapable of holding the group safe or making connections with the individuals in the group.

This is also the answer to "the fear of public speaking."

Get high enough on the SUE Scale, and there is no fear.

In the contrary.

There is a high desire to communicate with the group.

- **Leading a group becomes an exciting experience which is powerfully uplifting to the leader.**

There is still more.

In the old systems which disconnected teachers from their students through an impenetrable hierarchy, we have a situation where essentially, teachers and students are at war.

The teachers and students wrestle and struggle for power (for energy, for which all of them are desperate, and starving!) and in that battle, learning anything at all loses out and is forgotten.

When the students begin to understand that the best teacher they could possibly hope to have is an energized teacher, they can help the process unfold from their end.

Giving the teacher positive attention and feedback, for example, will lift the teacher - and the teacher will become a better teacher in turn.

It's an extraordinary thing.

It's simple and in practice, astonishing, profound, transformative.

Here is a real life example from a student on the MSM distance learning course of this theory in action.

> I was booked on what I thought was going to be a really interesting course about energy in my home town.
>
> I was looking forward to it - huge expectations!
>
> The trainer was not what I had expected, she didn't really know much about working with energy for real. I could feel my energy dropping and getting quite angry. I realised I had two possibilities. I could show her up for being weak on her theory, wrong about many things and increase her already significant stress and discomfort, or to try "The Seed" from my MODERN Stress Management course.
>
> I tuned in with my intention to look for the best in the trainer, had respect for her and for her current knowledge. I decided to support her - she was an older woman, had lived for a long time I felt that she could know things of value for me.
>
> Her response was instant. She felt my respect, my support and there was no fight! She gave the best of herself on this course, her inner wisdom was in action! We found common ground, common words. She learned, I learned. The whole group learned. Our trainer felt well and safe.
>
> We all supported each other in this group. Interesting was that she went away from the original focus of this course and gave people more of herself, her own discoveries from her own journey through life. We all were energized and enjoyed the course.
>
> After all it was fantastic! A great experience for me!

Imagine what would have happened if this person had not been present at this course and applied the simple principles of Modern Stress Management.

With the stress chart in hand, and applied to groups, it becomes easy to have better learning experiences.

It becomes easy and natural for the students to learn far more than just facts and data; for the teacher it becomes possible to be able to transmit the invisible parts of their knowledge, their wisdom, their understanding, their love of the subject. For both, the learning experience and the student/teacher interaction becomes an absolute joy that enriches both their lives.

From such learning experiences, people individually come away delighted, inspired, and most of all, ready for action in the real world.

I wish from the bottom of my heart that every teacher in the whole world would see, just for one moment, just once in their lives, a full stress chart.

I wish from the bottom of my heart that they would then start to see how the dynamics in their groups really work; what effects the highly stressed members of their groups are having; what activities bring the students up, what activities bring them down.

I wish they would apply it to themselves and start to realise when they are getting stressed, and taking steps to get themselves out of stress as quickly as possible, and on the right side of the SUE scale once more.

Just this one thing would completely transform the "experience of learning" for everyone concerned and start our youngsters on a whole new path in life.

Well, and as to the youngsters ...

Of course, we need to teach our children about stress.

About their stress, but also the ability to perceive it in other people, and to react accordingly.

"No, mummy doesn't hate you, and daddy is not completely insane. They act like that when they are too stressed ..."

The younger they are when they understand this, the more profound and cumulative the benefits across their lifetime will be.

Just take a moment and have a reflection on how different your own life would have been, dear reader, if your teachers had been less stressed, if your parents had been less stressed. If you had known where your weird performance failures in mind, body and spirit had come from. If you had known any of this.

Think about your childhood. Think about your youth. Think about your tweens and your teens.

Wow ...

What different lives we might have led ...

Imagine me breathing a deep sigh here.

As always, that was the old.

We have a chance for the new.

And, in the meantime, just remember this.

The higher you are on the SUE Scale, the more powerful you feel and the more powerful you become.

Your energy system literally expands and reaches further, can encompass more and more spheres of influence.

That's the direct opposite of the "Dying Process" where the spheres of influence collapse in on themselves until there's only one person remaining.

In groups, naturally the people with the brightest energy systems become the leaders. As the people with the most damaged/darkest/neediest energy systems are the ones who are being picked on so they will leave the group and stop bringing the party down.

If you don't think of yourself as a "natural born leader," think again.

In the country of the blind, the one eyed man is king.

As it stands in the world today, people have no idea that they even have an energy system.

You only need to raise your own energy to +3 and people will notice and comment how you seem more handsome, more beautiful, more attractive ...

It's not hard.

And the converse is true also.

Never try to lead anyone or anything unless you're on the right side of the SUE scale. Chances are, you'll lead them to defeat rather than victory. What with the whole short sightedness, uncontrollable emotions, loss of intelligence and all of that ...

Add energy into the equation, and it all makes sense, becomes easily explained, but most of all, it gives us practical ways to improve the situation almost instantaneously.

Your Happiness Matters

Now of course I don't know who you, my dear and dearly beloved reader, are.

Not who you are now, nor who your future aspects might be when they hit plus ten - the "really real you."

But I can tell you this:

<u>Your happiness matters.</u>

It matters a lot more than you think it does.

Because at the energy levels, we're not as separate as we think we are.

Energy bodies can make connections, and form larger entities, I call them "bubbles."

The most obvious one is the couple bubble.

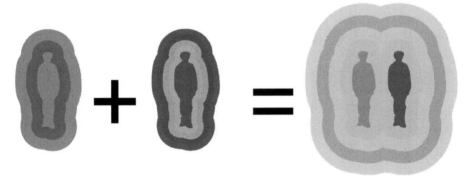

This can happen between two people at any time and may or may not be sexual in nature; and it's not just a connection like a hosepipe going from one person to the other, it's much more than that.

- **Their energy systems combine to form a whole new entity which is more than the sum of its parts.**

Inside this bubble, energy travels around freely.

This is why couple bubbled people think, feel and say the same thing at the same time; have "telepathic" incidents and other strange phenomena which you can't explain in the world view where everything is made of rock, but which is immediately and blatantly obvious when you *learn to think energy.*

People are designed to bubble with others of their own species, or any species that will allow such things.

So people couple bubble with dogs, and with horses, and those who don't or can't couple bubble with social mammals will ever know just how amazing it is to be a part of such an expanded entity where both become uplifted, and more than the sum of their parts.

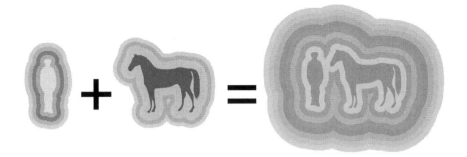

"Why do some people experience human-like bereavement when their dog dies? They must be crazy ..."

Yeah, well ...

People are social mammals by design, and by design, they're supposed to bubble, to combine their energy systems with others, form a partnership, form a group, form a tribe, an entity that is more than the sum of their parts.

These bubbles have many advantages, but they also have the disadvantage that everyone in a bubble gets infested by the stress of a single individual.

That lowers the total SUE state of the bubble, and now the bubble itself becomes more stupid, more clumsy, more short sighted and more emotionally unstable in direct response.

In high schools, the army and old people's homes, stressed individuals are attempted to be excluded from the group bubble. This is also known as "bullying" and an attempt by the bubble to drive unwanted individuals away, so that the bubble stays strong. You could think of it as an immune system response, it is as structural as that.

In a monkey tribe, living in a vast rain forest, that's not a problem.

The affected individual will simply leave.

In human situations, both they and the group who is desperate to exclude them are forced to stay together and ... well ... it's a sad, sad story.

You can legislate against the "five sense visible" tip of the iceberg bullying, but the real stuff happens at the energy levels, and for energy reasons.

117

When we are looking at people's behaviour in groups, adding our 16.7% of energy awareness connects the dots, yet again.

There are many different results of this.

Proper stress awareness isn't just about assessing the stress of the individual, although that is where it all starts.

Indeed, when we assess the stress of an individual, we always ask the question, "Who is that person bubbled with, and what are their stress levels?"

Having a "stress bunny" in your household is the perfect example of this.

Just one person in a family who is constantly highly stressed will bring the whole family bubble down the SUE Scale, big time.

Just one person in a department, in a squadron, in the board room, in the school class who is highly stressed will affect everyone who comes in contact not only with them, but with anyone from that bubble.

It goes further still.

A single man, living on his own, highly stressed, in a single day, can significantly affect everyone he comes into contact with - from a shop assistant to a tele-sales person, his neighbours, the postman, the people on the internet forum where he trolls ...

And the shop assistant has kids, the tele-sales person a mother and father, his neighbours have grand kids, the postman has a family, and he's a member of the local darts team, and the people on the internet forum are getting angry and stressed all over the world ... and they all have kids, and friends, and people they interact with ...

This goes through the roof when the single stressed individual is a manager, an entrepreneur, a team leader, a CEO, a general, a prime minister, a dictator ...

Indeed, the energetic connections are so vastly intertwined, and the results of stressed people ripple so extraordinarily far and wide, that I have brought it down to this simple statement.

<u>Your happiness matters.</u>

It is of the essence that YOU should make every effort you can to get out of stress as fast as possible, and get yourself higher on the SUE scale.

Your happiness matters.

It is of the essence that YOU should make every effort you can to get out of stress as fast as possible, and get yourself higher on the SUE scale.

Of course it is of the essence for your own health and sanity, for your life and what kind of life you will have lived by the time you lie on your death bed.

Of course it is.

But it goes so much further than that.

- **You affect all your bubbles.**

Much more so than you might believe at this time.

It is extraordinary what happens to couple bubbles, family bubbles and team/work bubbles, even huge entity bubbles such as the whole of New York city, or all of Europe, when somewhere, one individual starts to make their own happiness the No. 1 priority of their daily doings, and starts raising their energy levels.

- **Anyone who gets above +5, even only once in a while, becomes a stone thrown into a pond that ripples out and touches many, many other people.**

This isn't about preaching to others about stress - it's about actually having more energy, BEING a higher person.

To make that the goal, above all else, and to understand that whatever you or I or anyone wants out of life, we cannot achieve this whilst we're on the wrong side of the stress chart.

We have been wrongfully taught that we need to put everyone else's happiness before our own, and then we somehow get rewarded for a lifetime of servitude and martyrdom.

The service of an unhappy, stressed, miserable person isn't worth having. It produces energetic poison that serves no-one at all, not even those who are deserving of something wonderful but receive essentially, nothing at all.

It is only when you are on the right side of the SUE scale that you actually have something precious and valuable to give that helps other people.

This is why your happiness matters, and matters ENORMOUSLY.

I believe that only once we've truly understood this, we can go on to the next step which says ...

"Their Happiness MATTERS."

"They" can be anyone at all.

Anywhere in the world.

They can be your wife or your customer; your child or your cat, if you're couple bubbled with it, then its happiness matters to you, and the happier it is, the happier you will be.

Somewhere we need to learn and understand this principle, that "their" happiness really matters.

Including the poor, the homeless, the people in prison, the old, the disabled, the lonely.

"Yes," we nod, "Yes, that's what the prophets of the ages have been saying, that makes sense when you think in terms of energy.

"All these unhappy people have contact with policemen, prison wardens, social workers, nurses and carers, and they will carry that stress into their families, into our shops, onto our streets, into our society and it will affect us all ..."

Right.

But we need to go further.

Their happiness matters, that includes everyone.

Even ... deep breath now ... bankers.

Politicians.

Super rich people.

The Royal family.

Tax inspectors.

Bailiffs.

Parking vultures. Sorry, I meant Parking Enforcement Officers.

But it goes even further than that still, and now you really need to put your hands on your heart of energy and take a deep breath.

Their happiness matters.

This includes *everyone*.

Paedophiles.

Terrorists.

"The enemy."

"Those awful people who ..."

When you look at it structurally, and by this I mean energetically, systemically, logically, then the only way out of stress and into success for humanity at large is to take the mysterious "pursuit of happiness" very, very seriously now.

Just one stressed person can bring a whole village to its knees.

Find a way to de-stress them, re-energize them, and love and logic must prevail.

"I have a dream ..."

Well yes.

We all do.

Various ones, at that, depending on your stress levels at the time.

At -7, we dream of nuking everyone who has ever pissed us off. Of course we do.

At +7, we start dreaming very different dreams, and more than that, we become a whole lot more realistic.

Real reality can only be known at +10 ...

Let's start somewhere.

Let's start with YOU.

And your real understanding now that **YOUR HAPPINESS MATTERS.**

Make the pursuit (and eventual capture, and possession, but most of all, experience of) **your happiness your goal**.

MODERN Stress Management

So now, we finally have MODERN Stress Management, which includes that additional magical 16.7% of information about emotions and the energy body.

I've called it MODERN Stress Management MSM to delineate it from "the aged and wrong stress management," all those programs based on the old shocked rat rubbish research from 1908 about classic conditioning.

I've written the training programs, the handouts, the brochures and I am writing this book.

I am immersed in MSM.

A couple of days ago, I went to the dentist's.

Whilst we were sitting, waiting for the injection to take affect, the dentist asked me, "So have you written any new books lately?"

I launched straight into the Modern Stress Management story, how over a hundred years ago, they used to shock sleeping rats, and if they didn't shock them enough, they would go back to sleep, and if they shocked them too much, they would go completely berserk, and if they shocked them in the middle, they would panic, try and run away and complete the maze eventually.

And how that is just useless for people, and how it led to this stupid idea that "some stress is good for you."

The dentist nodded and said, "Yes, I've heard that, lots of times. Never liked it, really ..."

"That's right," I said with passion, "It's bullshit! No stress is good for you! You need positive emotions to function the best you can!"

"These guys back in the day never tried sending happy rats through the maze - they would have outperformed the stressed rats in every way, from how fast they learn the maze to how long they would remember the layout! Happy rats simply do better at everything!"

At which point, the young female dental nurse, who was sitting on a stool in the corner, squealed out, "I want to be a happy rat!"

We all exploded in laughter at this - so my dental treatment began with high energy, and as it happened, was finished in 30 minutes rather than the allocated 45 minutes.

"Strange," said the dentist when I sat up and looked at the clock, "That went really smoothly, really well."

And I thought, yes, well, you've just demonstrated the happy rat principle, right here. Everything works better, faster, nicer, smoother, more flowing and more elegantly when you have good energy levels.

So yes.

MODERN Stress Management.

Every single person I told the rat story to, and there have been many, most of them absolute civilians like the dentist and the nurse, they understand.

They get it.

And they're excited by it.

Of course!

Permission to not be stressed and seek positive emotions, seek happiness instead.

Of course, it makes sense.

I'm going to conclude this "energy quick start" manual with some easy ways you can start being happier more often, stop energy drops and stress slides, and learn for yourself what sort of performance improvements you can get when you're firing on a few more cylinders.

If you are suffering from long term, ongoing chronic energy body stress, usually due to such things as having energy body injuries from having been in accidents, operations (where the physical body was stitched up/nailed back together but the energy body remains entirely untreated), energetic trauma such as having been in a plane crash, in a war, victim of crime, rape, battery and abuse, emotional mistreatment, bullying, loss and bereavement, and all those things which significantly affect the energy body, and for which neither medicine nor "psychology" offers any kind of useful treatment, I would advise you to see a modern energist as soon as possible.

The energy body can heal and it can be healed, but it requires energy body centred treatments, obviously.

Modern energists - members of the Guild of Energists - work simply, logically and without any psycho-babble with the real problems in the energy system. We don't use ancient oriental models, and we don't use needles. We work with energy - that's the right tool for the job.

I really do encourage people with severe energy body problems to seek the correct treatment for this, which of course is energy healing, as soon as possible. You really have suffered enough. Your problems are "not just all in your mind," they are real, and they hurt you. Just because they're invisible doesn't mean they aren't real. Modern energists understand this and act accordingly.

And here's the "government health warning" we must always add - modern energists deal with energy body problems only. We don't deal with physical problems, or "psychological problems." It is at this time actually very difficult to tell what is what, so I take the tack to give energy work a go. It doesn't cost much, and if the problem goes away, we know it was an energy body problem. If it doesn't, we know it wasn't. No harm, no hurt, just additional information we can use to find a different approach to the problem.

For most other people, simply becoming "energy aware" and acting accordingly, even just some of the time, will significantly reduce energy body stress and make you be happier, more often.

What always happens next is that we become more energy aware as regards our nearest and dearest.

We also start to notice how other people behave, and have a better explanation than, "He's just a bastard," - "She's just stupid," - "They are just insane."

That makes reality a better place to be.

A more logical place to be.

Eventually, it allows us to try out new things with people, to behave and respond differently.

And that's the way forward ...

Practical Changes

Carry a SUE Scale around with you or wear a SUE Scale wristband for at least a month and start taking notice of your stress levels.

Become consciously aware of the situations, times and places when your energy levels plummet down into the dangerous negatives.

After a while, you will notice patterns and when you do, you can make practical changes.

Here are just a few examples of how useful it is to learn yourself, and then go on to make practical changes that are right for you.

A couple on holiday had a husband in the couple bubble who knew about MODERN Stress Management. He noticed after five days that they would fight if they skipped breakfast in order to get out of the hotel fast to see attractions, but if they did take the time to have breakfast, not only were there no fights, they felt close and loving and this got better as the day progressed, ending in very good nights as well. He pointed this out to his wife. She immediately recognised the validity of his observation - and the rest of the holiday went swimmingly.

A man in "anger management" began to notice that he was always at his worst immediately after visiting friends in the old part of town where he had grown up. He also noticed that there was a significant drop in his energy levels as soon as he went past a row of shops that led to a street corner where he had many traumatic experiences as a child. He said, "I had never noticed this before, my energy levels dropped instantly and I like became this other person, always angry, always so confrontational. And then I'd bring that home with me. And the fighting would start." He decided to ask his best friends to come visit him at his house instead for now. "Not going there, the change it made, it was unbelievable. It really is like I can be a good person here, but not there."

What is important about this is that the man had fully believed "he was born bad" prior to learning about MSM. Now, there's every opportunity to work something out and keep his energy levels up, even when visiting the old parts of town. Eventually, he'll stay strong everywhere.

The owner of a small company noticed that the staff meetings would start out well, but then descended into arguments every time. He said, "After a while, I could actually feel it in my stomach when the energy started to drop." He noticed that this would be happening about half an hour into the meeting. He tried something different - he stopped the meeting which was still going well at 25 minutes and let the staff take an "outdoor break" for five minutes. When they came back in, they were laughing and smiling, and the meeting concluded without any arguments and in full agreement. "This is is such a simple thing, with such profound repercussions," he said.

A lady entrepreneur realised during a basic MSM course that she had been trying to do marketing from high stress states - and produced confusing marketing materials that "stank of desperation." She said, "By simply making sure I was high before I got on the keyboard, and immediately stepping away from the console when I noticed I wasn't in a fit state to be selling anything to anyone, I have found certainty in marketing! I know what I'm doing, and the results are awesome! This is so exciting! Oh how I wish I'd known this years ago!"

There was the programmer who beat himself up for a pattern he already knew - he would be able to concentrate on his work for so long, but then he would find his thoughts drifting and he would "have to" visit a porn site and spend some time there, before he was ready to go back to work. "It was like a revelation," he said. "Concentrating that hard for that long and ignoring everything, including my body, that caused my energy to drop. When it got too low, I couldn't concentrate any longer, and looking at sexy pictures brought me back to life! Makes perfect sense! Now I take breaks every 45 minutes, look at a few pictures, feel better, back to work. And without the guilt! Not only have I nearly doubled my productivity, there are far fewer mistakes that I have to go back and fix. Brilliant!"

And there was the lady trainer who felt drained, exhausted and "wishing she was dead" after spending a full day in a classroom environment. After taking the MSM course, she said, "I can't tell you the difference it makes to not only realise when my own energy levels are going down, but when the whole group becomes stressed and disconnected. I've now added things that raise energy, simple things like talking about something positive, getting people to work together more, stopping more often to drink water - the difference it makes is absolutely amazing. The days go so much faster, the feedback from the students has improved dramatically - and I still have energy when I get home. Absolutely fantastic!"

There was an older gentleman who had to go to his bank in person. This got him very annoyed, but then he realised that he was simply stressed at the idea. He also realised that this was because the last five times he'd been to that bank he had had seriously bad experiences. He had been treated with disrespect, and never gotten the help he wanted before. So he decided to test out the high energy theory, rather than entering into therapy first to deal with all the traumatic experiences at the bank. He asked himself what would keep his energy high, no matter what, and his granddaughter came to mind. He asked if he could borrow her for an hour, and of course, the mother was only too happy to let her go with him. "My granddaughter is a ray of sunshine. You just can't be down when you're with her. We went to the bank and played games while we were waiting in the queue. Other people got involved as well and we were all laughing and beaming by the time we got to the advisor. The advisor was enchanted by my granddaughter too and everything went well. The advisor was really helpful and found a way to get done what I wanted. We walked out of there like kings and queens! When I told my granddaughter how much she'd helped me, and thanked her sincerely, she was beaming."

What all these examples have in common is that the people in question worked it out all by themselves.

This is enormously different from prescribing one technique that everyone has to do, and some like it, some don't, some can't see the point in the first place.

Teaching people the basics about the energy body, about emotions, about low energy causing malfunctions in mind, body and spirit, this is what enables normal people to find their own solutions.

This is a perfectly uplifting spiral - the more energy you have, the clearer your thinking becomes, the more you are able to see what's there, find new inspiration, new ideas, new solutions.

Plus, you have the energy required to carry out these insights into action.

Which leads to less stress ... more energy ... even more understanding, insight ... even better, even more practical ideas ...

It is this upward lifting spiral once you get people out of stress, and over that dead zone around Zero, which represents the true heart of The Trillion Dollar Stress Solution.

What Happens Next?

I am hoping that you, dear reader, will use the suggestions in this book to start looking at people with the SUE Scale and the Energy Body Stress Chart in mind.

I am also hoping you will look across your life and notice what happened when your past aspects were stressed, and when they were full of energy (if ever they were).

I am hoping that you are making those all important connections in your own mind and that you will begin to notice the reality of "energy in action" quite literally everywhere.

I am sincerely hoping that you will use what you have learned here to have a much better life - and much more interesting, expansive goals for the future!

I am also hoping that at least some of you will fall in love with energy, and become modern energists - people who have that additional 16.7% information in their awareness and who use this to their benefit, and the greater good.

In the old fashioned terminology, that would be enlightenment.

Becoming aware of the REALITY of energy is what enlightenment is.

Energy adds the WOW to everything, and offers amazing opportunities for personal development.

What has happened in the past is that anyone who understood a little bit about energy immediately started a cult, or a secret society, hoarding and hiding "the energy secrets of the ages" for power, control, profit and gain.

What I need and want to happen now is that people in general get back with the program and become energy aware - taking the power back to themselves, quite literally, empowering themselves, and in so doing, stepping into what they were each born to be.

In the past, it was thought of anyone who attained a random +10 at some point in their lives as a super hero, a prophet, a saint, a quirk of nature.

We now know that +10 is perfectly doable for normal people.

You just have to know it's there, that is has nothing to do with psychology or with physiology, that you don't have to sit on your ass in a monastery for 60 years staring at a blank wall to attain it.

Energy is real.

You can feel it in your body.

Take the simple SUE Scale and keep asking yourself, "What can I do to get higher? Even higher than that? Yes, and even higher than that, still!"

You will experience your own threshold shifts along the way - and that is finally, personal development that is real, lasting, personal, and essentially infinite.

What Is The Objection?

Something I can't explain is why there is so much resistance to adopting the simple thought model that people have a physical body, and they also have an energy body.

As we have discovered, it makes perfect sense and "explains people" beautifully.

It is a direct route to emotional mastery, and to better performance across the board.

All the people who ever did anything good for humanity knew about this, talked about this, and enacted it in some way.

Yet, in the Middle Ages the powers that be went on a massive drive to extinguish energy work in all its various guises (they called it witchcraft) in order to hold the monopoly on all and everything energy related.

Today, we have the Wiki Nerds, the modern incarnation of the old witch sniffers, who are in complete "Alchemy Denial[5]" as I've taken to call it, trying to stamp out anything that even remotely touches on working with the human energy body.

We also have the general witch hunt by "science" that is ongoing and which prevents anything energy body related being used to help us people feel better.

I would be amiss if I did not mention that we also have religions, banging on from the other side, who also want to stamp out any mention of energy work that is reasonable and logical.

You could turn this around and say, "Well, if they're all so desperate to stamp it out - then there must be something in it! Surely, if it was just all of us energists being crazy, you wouldn't need to get so upset and go on the war path like this ...?"

What is it about energy work that it frightens the living daylights out of "the powers that be" - and it doesn't seem to matter if that's in 12AD or 1455, or 2015?

Is it that people who have this secret, forbidden knowledge of the ages start to think for themselves?

That they can rise above the usual daily terrors, big, small, and entirely imagined, to find personal power, make up their own minds, and try to change the status quo?

Is that what it is?

Is it as simple as that?

---

5 *Alchemy Denial means that the typical Wikipedia contributor "forgets" to mention the fact that all the greats throughout history and including "the fathers of modern science" were also, to a man, all "alchemists" - studying esoterics and metaphysics, or working with energy, in other words. There isn't a single person throughout history who did something extraordinary that created change and is remembered who did not work with energy, by any other name. If you don't believe me, check it out for yourself. But don't use Wikipedia. They're in alchemy denial and try to make the facts disappear.*

Well, if it is, the World Wide Web has finally given us all an opportunity to find our own personal space of freedom and conduct our own investigations, one person at a time.

As I keep saying - don't take my word for it. That's the last thing I want, that's the old which has kept people entrapped and going around in ever decreasing circles with this idea that "other people know better than you do."

To the so-called sceptics, I would say this.

"Try this out for yourself.

"Be a proper scientist, a real scientist, not a brainwashed puppet that repeats the old just as furiously as any brainwashed religious fundamentalist.

"Take my theory and test it out.

"Take my thought model and test it out.

"If you can't or won't, don't dare call me "unscientific."

"I have as much right as anyone else to make a theory and run my own experiments. As yet, there is no law to forbid me to do this, or to think for myself.

"Take my theory, my models and run your own real life tests on it.

"Make up your own mind.

"But be sure to be energized, because as you know, below Zero you're just going to be more and more stupid, more and more illogical, more and more insane ..."

Everyone Dreams ...

I will freely admit that the approaches to try and work with energy which have existed in the past were deeply flawed and need to be replaced.

This goes from the "Ancient Oriental" systems (based on monks living 6,000 years ago, from a heavily ancestor worshipping agricultural based culture, men only, sameness driven, now irrelevant) to the well meaning "New Age" wibbly wobbly "subtle energy" nonsense, of which there is a lot about.

The problem has always been that people were trying to explain certain phenomena in the best way they could, based on personal experiences, and as soon as you do that, other people start to listen, because they too are looking for a way to conceptualise their own experiences somehow, and deal with their own energy system - somehow.

Everyone dreams.

It doesn't matter how long you force children to rock backwards and forwards while mumbling words from an old scroll and beat them with sticks if they stop.

They will still go home, and they will still love, and have fears, and thoughts, experience emotions, and they will dream.

For all the mistreatments, you can't beat being human out of a human being.

Sure, the more you beat them, the worse they get, and in the end, you end up with terrible human beings.

But even those terrible human beings still dream, and they still fall in love, and they still pray, and they still have hope for better ...

It's a complete tragedy, a complete disaster of epic proportions what is happening to people's energy bodies the world over.

I made it my business to focus on that forgotten, neglected part of the human totality that drives truly everything, from the cradle to the grave, in exclusion and without looking over my shoulder.

I decided to investigate the energy body, what it does, exclusively.

What this means is that I didn't come in with the view to try and "cure the physical body" via the energy body, for example.

I'm really not that interested in the physical body, as an investigative scientist of my age.

What you have in New Age witchcraft and New Age type of approaches is a last resort for those who didn't get anywhere with the pills and potions prescribed by their doctors. Or people who were disappointed by the results of endless psychotherapy which didn't seem to hit the mark at all.

What I say is that the energy body is foundational and important in its own right. It is so important because it runs emotions, and emotions run the world of men.

But I found that it does more than that. The energy body runs intelligence, creativity and logic as well.

That was a surprise.

When I found this, I realised that I had to do something more than just come up with a new technique for dealing with the energy body correctly.

I needed to go much further, and engineer an entire new field.

A true Third Field in the Mind, Body, Spirit triad.

A field that deals with the human experience of the mysterious energy worlds and our own energy bodies.

Modern energism.

I started literally with Tabula Rasa - from the ground up.

Which produced one of my favourite diagrams of all times - my diagram of the human energy body.

So the theory goes, "We have an energy body."

But what else do we know about it?

If we completely clear our minds of all the old stuff about nadis and chakras and meridians, and thin men sitting in the lotus position, staring at walls ...?

How can we know what the energy body is doing?

Well ... and that led us straight to the emotions, the 6th sense, the energy body stress chart ...

And here we are, with The Trillion Dollar Stress Solution.

The diagram above is truly, the only diagram we should ever make of any energy body - yours, mine, his and hers.

We have no idea how even a perfectly functioning energy body should or could be mapped (we can't see it, can't measure it, and we certainly shouldn't take other people's words for it that THEY have somehow seen it and that's what it looks like. Just in case they are a) lying or were b) high on some substance when they "saw" it!).

I am guessing that this far into the book, we don't have the people any longer who totally HATE the concept or even the possibility of there being such a thing as an "energy body" (or a human "spirit," or any of the other words that have been used over the ages).

These people would have thrown the book away in disgust a long time ago.

For those of us who had the good sense to stay with it, and read on, I say this.

The very idea that there could be an energy body changes your life.

But it truly only changes your life for the better if you then go on to keep living life with that big question mark.

Don't buy into the old systems.

Use your own intelligence, ask your own questions.

There is a mother screaming at her little 3 year old girl in a supermarket.

If both mother and child had energy systems, what would be happening here?

There are a bunch of fanatics rioting, screaming, dancing around burning effigies.

If they all had energy systems, what would be going on there?

Here's a person who is suffering from PTSD.

If they had an energy system, what might be happening right now?

Once you ask that questions, answers will reveal themselves to you.

Cause and effect ***connections***.

Huge, and I mean HUGE, "Aha!!!" effects on a daily basis.

And that's where we start with MODERN energism.

With questions, with reality, with what we can actually notice all around us, with our own personal investigations.

I am sincerely hoping that folk won't now go on and mess it all up again, and go down that path the old Orientals did, by drawing more and more complicated, useless maps of idealised energy systems that never existed at all and in the first place.

Think about that.

What good is a map that pertains to a place which doesn't exist, and never has, when you're trying to get a ship to shore?

It's no good at all.

You are a million times better off (more successful, less endangered, safer, righter, better!) by throwing the map away and observing what's really around you.

People's energy bodies are in all sorts of states.

People have injuries in their energy systems from way back when, starving, stressed energy bodies, unhappy energy bodies with broken hearts ... it's actually scary once you start to pay attention.

We really need this energy awareness, we need modern energism, to sort this mess out.

To start a revolution to make people feel better.

"The powers that be" don't want this. They like to keep the people at a constant -4 so they won't ask too many questions and run like the rats through the maze, blindly, constantly terrified, producing endless wealth for those who control them at the cost of their own lives lived to their full potential.

The powers that be don't want the big energy secret to get out.

I say "the people" do.

I believe that we need to draw a firm line under whatever insanity existed in the past, take a deep breath, and start afresh, from the ground up, with MODERN energism.

Where modern, intelligent, literate people, which includes, for the first time in the history of humanity, also women (!), begin an intelligent discussion on what we can do to put things to rights, put an order and sequence into action that acknowledges the reality of human beings as having both a material as well as an energetic existence.

Humanity absolutely needs "The Third Field."

The "Third Field" is the spirit in the mind, body, spirit triad.

But it's not some ghastly nonsense - it's the energy body, a functional reality, a fact of life.

Without acknowledging the existence of the energy body, we are going to go around in ever decreasing circles as the men of the world get ever more stressed, madder, and both their desire as well as their ability for mechanical destruction grows and grows.

I read the other day that there was a useless warplane being manufactured at the cost of one trillion dollars (note the "useless"!) when in the same breath the meagre subsidies for children in poverty are cut in order to "save money."

That's insanity in action.

This has to stop.

We're not going to stop it with a wonder pill the chemists cook up; we're not going to stop it with yet another religion to fight about.

We will certainly never, ever stop it by sitting around, watching the "Terror Alert" being raised yet again, and feeling hopeless, powerless, and desperately stressed.

There is next to nothing we can personally do to make "the powers that be" change their crazy courses of action.

We can however, do something about our own energy bodies and take control of our own stress levels, one person at a time.

That is a power we do have.

That is more power than we ever dreamed of, because when we get on the right side of the SUE scale, we literally become that centre that causes the ripples in the pond to spread out far and wide, affecting everyone we come into contact with.

It starts with us, and the beneficial effects spread to our loved ones, our friends, our colleagues, our customers.

Each one of us has the power to change our own worlds, and together, eventually, the entire world will change.

Modern energism has no religion. It has no political affiliations and most of all, it's not owned by a bank or a giant chemical corporation.

It is simple, it's here, and we can use it free of charge, right now.

We can use it to make our own lives a better place.

It's simply a question of factoring in that magical, missing 16.7% information and start applying what we learn in our businesses, in our families, in our churches, in our relationships.

We just need to get over our own entrainments, reversals, brain washing, perceived limitations and that god awful glass ceiling of Zero.

Now, I can't do this alone - I need YOUR help!

I need you to rise above the fear and talk about the reality of energy freely where ever it needs to be talked about.

I need you to pass on this book to a person who is stressed and needs to read this, urgently. When they've read it, charge them with passing it on to someone else to whom it would make all the difference.

I need entrepreneurs to go ahead and use what they have learned to move themselves and their businesses from stress to success, simply by making sure they don't take desperate or silly actions and decisions from stressed states any longer.

I need a few visionary business persons, perhaps like the one we started out with, who have it in his or her power to say the word, and all their 2, 20, 200, 2000 or 20,000 employees get a one hour lesson in MODERN Stress Management.

A SUE Scale and an Energy Chart to take home, to try out, to think about.

That would break the spell, to throw off the old brain washing and enact an energy body based approach to less stress, more productivity, less mistakes, less churn, more success.

Or in other words, a better bottom line.

We can look at those companies and their performance, in black and red, before and after.

We will see a predictable result.

It doesn't matter if this is happens in China, in Germany, in the UK, in the US, in India, in Singapore, in Australia.

It doesn't matter because all human beings have energy bodies, and they will all improve when their energy levels go up.

MSM is that structural, it is that systemic.

Then we can show the results to the other business owners, the ones who are too stressed to think for themselves, too scared, too nervous, too terrified and need to wait for validation, for others to go first. Then, they too will come around and avail themselves of what is an absolutely astonishing competitive advantage in their markets and their fields.

What would a race team give for a 16.7% increase in their performance?

What would a company give for a 16.7% increase in profits?

Well ... that's the Trillion Dollar question.

Let us not forget that "stress relief" isn't what MSM is all about.

It's about true optimal performance.

That's vastly different.

Everyone is looking for a bit of water to put out a raging fire, just so they have some smoking ruins, a bit of "peace" and can think of rebuilding.

That's the old.

We are in the new, and we are talking about a wave that transforms everything it touches.

Ladies, gentlemen and all others - I invite us all to finally come out of the Dark Ages, and step into a better future.

A more logical future. A more reasonable future. A more loving future. A more intelligent future.

It's there.

Now we simply have to go and do something about it.

One person at a time.

Calling On The Power Of The People

What I find extraordinary is that my approach to modern energism manages to piss off every one of the current "powers that be."

Of course, we have the usual suspects who hate anything that isn't theirs - the so called scientists, the people on the autistic spectrum who can't handle emotions at all, which comprises the vast majority of the new "priest cult of the techno nerds," the vested interest people who don't want to re-do their ancient studies and re-write their ancient manuals, the vested interest groups who want control of psychology, of medicine, of pharmaceuticals, of screwing money and more money out of people into their own pockets, with never an end in sight.

We have all the establishments, which love to do the same things they have always done and will cling to the old, like the hapless passengers clinging to the rails of the Titanic as she goes down.

We have all the vested interests in religion, which is at the end of the day, also only about taking power and money from the people now, no matter what they like to say and no matter how truthful and revolutionary their founding prophets may have been once upon a time.

We even have all the vested interests of the New Age, who love their unicorn illusions and waffle on about subtle energy, prana and chi, chakras and all that jazz without having much or any connection to any actual reality in the process.

It was true that after years upon years of trying to get someone, somewhere to see the light, I was getting extremely despondent and hopeless.

I have to admit that on many occasions I just wanted to give up.

People seemed to be totally stuck on their fairy stories of mystic symbols handed down from some burning bush, or total rejection of the simple logic of modern energism on the grounds that it would bring demons up from hell, or that it was too unscientific, which is completely ridiculous.

I had a bizarre experience with one of my trainees running an energy based course in a school in the UK. Nothing esoteric, simple EMO.

"When you get bullied, where do you feel the emotional pain in your body? Show me with your hands," that kind of thing.

The children benefited tremendously, as they would; the teachers were delighted. But then the school board found out about it, came down like a ton of bricks on the headmaster, and the program was immediately cancelled. This was reported in the press, and some professor of chemistry was trotted out to denounce the system as witchcraft. The man had no idea what the system was, had never read the book, had no information whatsoever - but he denounced anyway.

I hope he was paid well.

Modern energism threatens the status quo.

This is a fact, and I was about to give up on many occasions. A near final straw came with the aggressive and hate filled attacks of the Wikipedia nerd-force on EFT. It seems we just couldn't win, no matter that over 10,000 people, including hundreds of medical, psychiatric and psychology PhDs, signed the petition, pleading to have simply fairer treatment for EFT on Wikipedia.

Jimmy Wales, Founder of Wikipedia, responded on 23 Mar 2014 with:

> *No, you have to be kidding me. Every single person who signed this petition needs to go back to check their premises and think harder about what it means to be honest, factual, truthful.*
>
> *Wikipedia's policies around this kind of thing are exactly spot-on and correct. If you can get your work published in respectable scientific journals - that is to say, if you can produce evidence through replicable scientific experiments, then Wikipedia will cover it appropriately.*
>
> *What we won't do is pretend that the work of lunatic charlatans is the equivalent of "true scientific discourse". It isn't.*[6]

The work of "lunatic charlatans" ...?

That's the sort of thing you come out with at -7 and it really doesn't sound too scientific, does it.

No emotional mastery there ...

Unlike him, we can do something about our negative emotions. We can raise energy if we need to. We can do this using modern energy techniques such as EFT, or EMO. We can also do this by directing our mind to focus on something we love, or simply by stepping outside for a moment, breathing the fresh air and enjoying the sunshine.

You can feel yourself coming back to life, coming back to your senses, becoming forgiving, compassionate and seeing the bigger picture once again.

At the time, I did just that and an idea came to me.

I needed to get away from the irrational, stressed out energy deniers.

They are the tiniest of minority, and they only seem so powerful because they make such a lot of noise.

There are over 6 billion people in the world.

I wonder what might happen if I addressed them directly ...?

That is when I decided to reach out to the people. Normal people. That's when I travelled thousands of miles for a whole year long and talked to normal people.

What I found, time and time again, is that real, normal people do want this information.

That it helps them significantly.

Normal people are more than interested in this piece of information that finally makes sense of their lives.

---

6   *There are to date 27 studies on the efficacy of EFT which have been published in a wide variety of scientific journals. Please see http://theamt.com/eft_studies.htm*

And I learned this.

This has to be a grass roots (r)evolution.

The old guard who doesn't want to re-write their training manuals will never be convinced by logic, or the truth.

For them, it's not about the truth.

It's about money. It's about power.

But even here modern energism trumps them.

Apply the principles, and you will make more money than they do.

That's not just in the context of stress relief.

The products you create, the machines you build, the systems you produce are better and more profitable. They are competitively superior, have a huge competitive advantage. Energy awareness puts a sparkle on everything it touches, and it is what people have always been hungering for, are hungering for right now.

This is why I turned away from the endless battle with the vested interests, and to the people who really work in the real world - normal people and business people, who have real lives, who want better performance, who know that they are capable of so much more, but simply didn't know what they had to do to get there.

Resolve the stress problem, and you have more intelligent people.

It's no wonder that the liars, cheats, charlatan, manipulators, propagandists, spinners and thieves don't want people to get their hands on this.

It's no wonder that this basic piece of knowledge - the reality of the human energy body! - has been kept a mystical secret that you have to spent all your life and all your savings on to have revealed in dark crypt of the last and final secret initiation.

But that is the old.

I'm done with it.

No more secrets. No more lies. No more deceptions. No more "opium for the people."

Definitely no "Brave New World."

The future will be different from the past when we simply add that little missing 16.7% into the equation.

The Modern Energist

As you might have guessed by now, dear reader, the SUE Scale, the Stress Chart and the fact that we are different people sequentially as we go through life and our energy bodies change their state, is just the tip of the iceberg.

Getting out of stress and into a more energized life is only the beginning.

There isn't a single field of human endeavour that can't be radically improved by taking the reality of energy exchanges into consideration.

I define the modern energist as a profession thus.

- **A modern energist is a person with the knowledge and experience to advise on the energetic components to any given situation.**

In the context of MODERN Stress Management, that would be to advise people how to get out of stress and into success by managing their energy states better.

This alone is priceless; it's worth a whole lot more than just a miserly trillion dollars.

Still, there is so much more.

There are a myriad of incidences relating to health and sanity where, without factoring in the energy body, you get absolutely nowhere.

In fact, and I have mentioned this already, even "scientific medical tests" that don't take the stress levels of their subjects into consideration, will have to produce very questionable results.

Indeed, any "scientific research" that doesn't deal correctly with the emotions and states of the subjects, but also of the researchers, is highly questionable.

A "scientist" who "hates the idea" that a new theory might be right will produce ... what kind of research ...?

We have already mentioned "psychology" - the field that is supposed to be "the science of the soul." (Psyche - The Soul, Logia - Reason or Reasoned Study, in Greek.)

Really ...?

I've seen what youngsters get to "study" when they enter into that field, even still in this day and age. And the term "soulless" springs to mind ... unless you're in love with statistics. Perhaps we should take a class action for wrongful labelling when there's an entire field of so called science actively fighting against the idea of the existence of that thing they're supposed to be studying?

We have crazy art. Crazy magic. Crazy health care systems. Totally crazy religions (even though some of their original founders, many thousand years ago, were probably on the right track and were trying to do much the same thing I'm trying to do now).

There isn't a single thing that can't be improved upon by getting a modern energist involved.

Modern energists aren't like the crazy magicians of old, or weird priests from secret sects, or the well meaning, lovely but ineffective New Age unicorn lovers.

Modern energists are people just like you and me, people who have seen the sense in being sensible, realistic, and working with what is really there right now, instead of looking to ancient scrolls and "laws" handed down from the veritable ancestors to explain how the world really works.

Modern energists address the human component in the equation.

This has never even been properly attempted before.

Which is a bit of a shocker, given we have ten thousand years of so called civilisation.

Well, never mind!

Let's turn away from the old, let's step into the new, eyes wide open, all senses providing us with useful information.

Get out of stress and into clarity, and I am now convinced that as a species, we are capable of the most wonderful things.

We might even turn out to be an asset to creation at large.

Now wouldn't that be something ...?

Practical Enlightenment

Enlightenment is when that additional 16.7% information clicks into place and the entire world transforms from this bewildering, hard, incomprehensible place to a veritable wonderworld - Zauberwelt, as I like to call it.

In the past, people would have experiences and randomly become enlightened.

With modern energism, anyone who would like to become enlightened can do so. Many people are already enlightened, they just don't know that they are.

Many people have already had experiences that convinced them "there's more between heaven and earth, Horatio .." than they were told about at school.

Without a framework of reference, it is hard to talk about these experiences.

The Energy Chart gives us this framework of reference.

Instead of enlightenment experiences or numinous experiences, we simply call them high positive events - and a true enlightenment experience is a +10.

We can even create +10s at will, for example, using simple EFT. You move up the SUE Scale, a round of EFT at a time, and if you keep going, eventually you will have that +10 event. Completely under your control, and on a topic of your choice.

As far as I know, that's unprecedented in the history of humanity.

We can go further than this and learn to raise energy in all sorts of ways, as we have discussed. With practice, +10s become perfectly achievable and they happen more and more frequently.

The enlightenment gets better, and brighter ...

The world and absolutely everything within it becomes more and more fascinating, more and more beautiful, more and more filled with awe and an astonishing sense of grace that permeates everything.

It is important for me to tell you that "stress relief" isn't the end of the story - but it is the beginning.

The beginning of a whole new story altogether, a better story, a very different story.

The energy worlds are endlessly fascinating and offer every opportunity to play, to learn, to engage, to nourish ourselves in a most wonderfully profound way.

Being an enlightened human being is a wonderful state of being.

We now need to know this, remember that there is a truly magical world we can enter into when we raise our energy levels high enough, and allow ourselves to become excited by this!

The Healing Path: The Journey To Love

Last weekend, I decided to attend the first book festival which had been organised in the town I live in.

After all these years of working with the Internet, promoting e-books since 1996 and running a thoroughly modern publishing company with employees, collaborators, authors and customers all over the world, I really felt I wanted to let the local people know that we are here.

All our books, manuals, courses and media sets are on MODERN energy work, which means they are based on understanding the Energy Body Stress Chart, the SUE Scale, and working with the reality of human emotions in the 21st century.

We have published very in-depth pure information books, required reading books for practitioners of modern energism, self help, how to, non-fiction. We have also published poetry, fantasy fiction, fairy tales and metaphor/story telling based books, in which language is used "with energy in mind."

To a person who hasn't heard of any of these things, that can be quite perplexing. There were those in the publishing company who said that it would be a waste of time and money as we would never sell enough books to the general public to pay for the stand and two people to be there all weekend.

I agreed with this assessment, and still wanted to do it anyway.

The great road trip had taught me the value of speaking to real people, in the real world; interacting with them, learning from them, listening to them. I have felt for a long time that we were too insular in spite of the global community of modern energists, and that we needed to get out there more.

So instead of hiring staff for the local book fair, the journal editor of The Energist and myself volunteered to give up our weekends to be present.

We took a few samples of our magazines, stress management brochures, the newly published Art Solutions colouring book, and our fiction and fantasy titles.

As an afterthought, I picked up my own copy of Infinite Creativity and The Genius Symbols on the way out the door and put them in my bag.

The book festival was lovely, wonderful people and we had a great time on the first day. As predicted, we sold few books but we met lots of people, made new local contacts and generally, spread a little happiness as we kept each other's energy high and did our best to raise other people's spirits in any way we could.

It is truly remarkable how simply the will to keep on the right side of the SUE Scale makes such an inordinate difference to ... absolutely everything.

To have a "good attitude" regardless of external circumstances is absolutely priceless.

To keep focused on raising energy is the answer to ... absolutely everything, yet again.

It is the answer to the problem of, "It's too hot in here!" Raise your energy, have a laugh, and you don't notice it any longer. It's gone. The problem has totally disappeared from your conscious awareness and your are doing other things instead of moaning, groaning, sweating and suffering.

Raising energy is the answer to, "I've been standing for too long and my feet hurt!" This too just goes away as your focus is drawn to something else altogether - a nice young lady who is interested in my books on creativity and genius. A wonderful conversation, a connection - nothing hurts any longer, in the contrary. I feel happy, young and strong.

It's the answer to the problem of, "There are not enough customers, we'll never earn enough to make it worth our while!" This very much depressed many of the other authors and publishers in the hall, making them struggle to be welcoming to the customers who were there. Raise energy by any means and all of a sudden, there are all sorts of opportunities for learning, for connection, for having fun.

And I did. I learned lots of things, especially just how incomprehensible our materials are to people who have no background in energy work, personal development, NLP, hypnosis, Reiki or anything that would create a bridge between their experience and what we are offering here.

So the next day, Stephen and I went even further. We made the decision to completely let go of any thoughts or intentions of "selling books" and to "make love your goal" our ONLY objective.

To raise energy in and with anyone who came to our stand today. To make them be happier, a little brighter, cheer them up. To practice that, to do that all day.

As I arrived at the venue, I found the organisers moving chairs and tables because some authors had decided not to return as they "had not sold a single book."

The organisers were upset by this, of course; I did my best to help, got our neighbouring stand, an author's collective with many people, a bigger space and somehow ended up with a long run of three tables for us at the end.

As I wondered how to put out our brochures and books, I had a moment of revelation.

I would organise what we do like a narrative - a journey.

I started putting the things relating to therapy and healing at the beginning, then the Modern Stress Management brochures. Next to those, I put the Art Solutions colouring in books, because people buy them for de-stressing; then the books on creativity and genius, then the poems, the fairy tales and the fantasy fiction titles.

Right at the end of the long run of tables, I put my large painting called "I come in love!" to finish off on the highest note, in keeping with, "Make love your goal!"

Now, we had a story.

Now, we could explain ourselves and our books to the people who came.

"You start with healing and therapy over there, then it's just stress management for normal people. As stress recedes, you become more interested in art and creativity, and your own personal genius wakes up. That leads to wonderful poems and stories, and pure art at the end."

Amazing. The whole context of what we do in three sentences! People understood it right away - it was great. I was so pleased and on many occasions throughout the day, I thanked my energy mind for the great idea of laying out the story practically in books on the table.

I asked Stephen to take a photograph of the arrangement before the customers arrived and when I looked at the picture the next morning I had another realisation - namely that our products follow the SUE scale perfectly.

I had laid out "The Healing Path" in products and services.

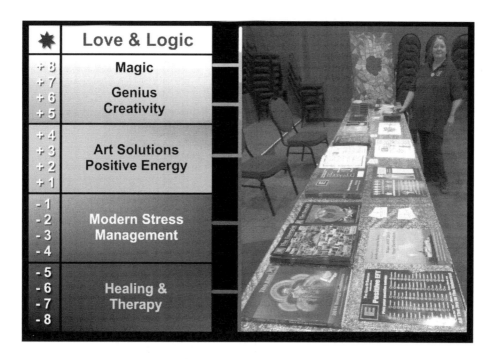

With the wisdom of hindsight, this is so obvious and seems so simple, but at the time it was a total revelation. It explained our customer's confusions, our own confusions, as well as what we have to do to get out of confusion and into clarity.

Now, we can simply ask customers what they are interested in, and direct them to the right products for the stage they are at in their personal journey towards love and logic, towards +10.

This diagram is also a bell curve, with the most customers to be found in the middle, between -4 and +4. Which explains perfectly why we always struggled to find customers for the high end creativity and genius products - it's out of reach and seems alien to those who seek healing, or stress management.

It gives me hope though. The more people we can move from stress and towards success, the more will "wake up" to their own inherent genius and creativity and then I'll have more people to play with, and do the things that I love doing best!

What I also love about this diagram is to see the outcome clearly - we are heading towards love and logic. That's the end result. To become more loving and to be more loved, without losing that all important clarity of mind, body and spirit I call "logic" and that I love so much, with all my heart.

Anyone who is in personal development, and many people who aren't, have wondered what they might be developing into?

Who do you want to be when you grow up?

The old role modes of trying to be like people who aren't you can never be anything but a distraction from your own true path.

I look at the picture and see that statement at the end, the painting with the hand and the rose, called, "I come in love."

I want to be me, my true self, and I want to understand love and logic. I want to feel it in my own body, I want to feel that grace that comes in these wonderful experiences when everything links up together, becomes more than the sum of its parts and I am right here, alive, present, and everything is simply beautiful.

This "Healing Path" or rather, "Journey To Love" is a fractal thing.

It is a big path as we raise our energy levels overall, the "base state" we inhabit most of the time moves up the SUE scale, becomes the new default.

But within that, there are shorter cycles that still follow the same progression which might last a few months, or a few weeks.

Within that, there are even shorter cycles and still, they follow the same progression. Every time you take a moment to raise energy, or when an EFT or EMO practitioner starts a session with a client who needs therapy and healing, we step onto that path and it always concludes in love and logic, if we follow through and go all the way to +10.

This fractal nature is to me the best proof that we are indeed, dealing with a natural system here - the design of the creative order shines through.

This is wonderful, and my decision to attend the small book festival in person, to essentially test the validity that "everything works better when you raise energy!" was rewarded beyond my wildest dreams.

Yes, we did sell books. Absolutely.

I got the most amazing feedback about my research, about my stories, about my art.

Before we arrived, nobody knew us. After the two days, I was asked to give the closing speech for the festival. I was delighted to do this and very honoured, too.

We learned things that will transform the way we do business from now on.

The value of this is literally incalculable.

146

Now take it to your own business, and your own life.

The key to success was to let go of the old goals ("We must sell books to make this worthwhile!") and to set goal to state instead - to literally, make love our goal.

The rewards were astonishing and included a master key to make our publishing company work exponentially better in every way.

Raise energy in any way you can, and your successes, your rewards, will blow you away.

From the bottom of my heart, I wish you to experience something like this too.

It is simply wonderful.

How To Die Happy

I spent many, many hours interviewing survivors of plane crashes and traffic accidents, as well as a whole raft of other "near death" scenarios.

I was particularly interested in that occurrence, so often described and talked about, when "your whole life flashes before your eyes."

I know how this works, because I have personally experienced it. Your life really does flash before your eyes - but not all of your life.

In those near death moments, what flashes before our eyes are _**only**_ the incidences of high positive energy.

Positive events, in other words.

What doesn't flash at all are long stretches of prolonged suffering. Insults and injuries. Misery and moments of trauma.

None of that seems to count for anything at all - it is only the high positives, the +10 events that are remembered in those nanoseconds when you are absolutely sure you are going to die now.

We can, as is usual, simply ignore this and say, well, it's just a massive outpouring of hormones, giving us hallucinations, nothing else.

Or we can say that it is an energy movement which results in an enlightenment experience.

The people to whom this has happened will all say the same thing.

They have changed their perspective on life.

They have understood how important LOVE is to their lives.

They have understood how precious our time is - and what we need to do to have had a good life when you die.

It is very simple, actually.

You don't die happy sitting on a mountain of stuff, like our friend Citizen Kane from the famous movie.

You die happy when you have had a life filled with a different kind of treasure - the +10 events.

Collect as many of those +10s as you can, and you will die happy.

When we work with energy and the SUE Scale, we can take control of our events - we can learn how to have these events, moments of grace and enlightenment, of love and connection which happen naturally when your energy system is firing on all cylinders.

I can tell you from my own experience and that of other modern energists that it becomes easier and easier to raise energy quickly and profoundly, in every day life.

It never ceases to amaze me how easy it is to become a much happier person - you just have to know those events exist in the first place; that you too are built to experience them; and that *we need to seek these events*.

We spend all our time seeking love and approval, and wanting stuff and more stuff and still more stuff, because we are seeking events.

To be fair, it is true that when I walked into the Mercedes Benz show room to collect my first ever (second hand!) Mercedes, it was an event for the aspect of that time.

The sales person who had sold me this car had understood this, and made a real effort to stage this from their side - I got a bunch of flowers, a plaque on a silver stand, the car lit in the middle of the showroom, with velvet ropes around it.

It was wonderful!

Yet it is only one event - and I have events all the time.

I can have a full on, full body event with droplets of rain in the grass, lit by the sun - I call this my "Daily Diamonds."

I can have an event being near my partner.

I had an event with a piece of home made chocolate at an artisan's faire - it was so good, it shuddered me through and through and I was on a high for the whole rest of the day.

I can have events anywhere, all the time - all I need to do is pay attention, set the process in motion, and make it so.

To be able to do that, I watch my stress levels. For sure, I am no angel, and I have my moments when I get angry, confused, freaked out, work too long, work too hard, get too obsessive with something.

My energy can go down rapidly and I can become a stress monster, just like everyone else.

But as time goes on, I am getting better and better at spotting the signs of stress and doing something right away that brings me back to the right side of the energy chart. I spend less and less time in stress, and more and more time on the sunny side of the street.

On the sunny side of the street, the raindrops sparkle. The colours are brighter, gravity is lighter and it is so much easier to become even happier than you already are - to ramp it up so that you have an actual EVENT.

A +10, an experience so powerful that it will be amongst those that flash before my eyes as I'm just about to die.

The +10 events is what people are actually seeking when they buy holidays, yachts, expensive outfits, tickets to a concert or a festival. Or wedding rings, for that matter.

If you understand energy, then you can disconnect from the material objects, the rituals such as "the best day in a woman's life is the day she gets married" (and

149

it's all downhill from there ...), from locations such as churches and sites of pilgrimage which promise events to be had.

You can then have your events there - but also here, right now, any time you choose.

That's true emotional freedom - to become aware of the invitations to have +10 events, wherever you go, and whoever you are.

I once had a client who was the survivor of extreme child abuse and had led a very difficult life. He wanted to know if he could ever be cured, if he could ever be normal.

I told him that the day he has collected more high positive events than the existing negative ones, his life would have been in summation more beautiful than it had been terrible.

At the time, I told him this to give him hope; in hindsight, my past aspect was right on the money.

It doesn't matter how much trauma you have experienced; if you still have the capacity to even just sometimes love a sunset, a kitten, a beautiful car or a beautiful person to the point that it makes you want to cry, you have the capacity for your own +10s still.

We simply didn't know how important the +10s were; some of us didn't even know they existed, and others had given up hope that they could ever experience such things.

With the energy chart in hand, we can re-claim our personal +10s.

When we do that, we totally transform our lives - and we will die happy. [7]

---

7   *Don't ever think it is too late now to stuff as many +10s as possible into your days and nights! Even if you are 99 years old, if you can still read this book, there's plenty of time to have more events than the people who don't know about the positive side of the energy chart ever will. Get started, head for the +10 with volition and all speed! Make your time count!*

The Trillion Dollar Stress Solution

The Trillion Dollar Stress Solutions is nothing more, and nothing less, than finally adding our essential 16.7% information about reality to our conscious constructs.

Or in other words, it means to become energy aware.

We can't see energy, but we can feel it.

We can also see (and hear, and feel!) the practical results of energy at work, energy in motion.

We can measure the effects of energy.

We don't know what "energy" "is" - but then we don't know what gravity is, either, and we can't see that, either. There are many things we don't know what they "are" but we can admit they exist because we can clearly notice the effects they are having.

Without energy awareness, people "make no sense." Not individually, not in a collection of many, not in sickness and not in health, either.

I encourage you now to start looking not for energy, but for its effects.

They are absolutely everywhere and give us the ability to take a whole new approach to the problems of the ages - and the problems facing each one of us, right here, right now.

- **The Trillion Dollar Stress Solution has to be enacted by clear thinking, visionary individuals who want to see positive change in the real world.**

We cannot afford for "science" to finally catch up; we cannot afford to wait for a new mathematics to emerge which can handle the complexities of how human beings actually work.

If we wait, we'll continue to waste our time, our money, our potential and our lives - just as all the stressed people who waited for permission to be happy have been doing for the last 10,000 years. People who were so stressed, they invented "World Religions" that hold you can't experience happiness until *after* you're dead!

I can't know about you, dear reader, but I'm no longer willing to hope that "the scientists" will finally come up with a happy pill and we all get to live in a Brave New World. By taking charge of our energy levels, and paying attention to our energy bodies, we get to take charge of who each one of us is - in the real world, in real time, in our real dealings with lovers, children, co-workers, employers and employees.

If what I have told you has made perfect sense to you, then act. Tell other people the good news.

"You're not crazy - you're just stressed."

Tell children who are failing in schools the good news.

151

"You're not stupid - you're just stressed."

Tell our bankers, politicians, policy makers and even our scientists, who are also people at the end of the day.

Stressed people make terrible decisions.

Stressed leaders lead stressed people into ever more problems.

Stressed law makers make appalling laws we all have to suffer from.

We need to get out of stress, and into success.

We need this on an individual basis, on a local basis, on a societal basis, on a global basis.

Most of all, tell everyone who will stand still for long enough the good news.

People are not born bad. They are being driven crazy by stress.

People are really capable of astonishing things - ALL people are.

Raise their energy levels, and the world will change.

It is as simple as that.

Ladies, gentlemen and all others - I give you ...

The Trillion Dollar Stress Solution.

Silvia Hartmann
September 1st, 2015

MSM In A Nutshell

If you are unused to the amazing ways of energy, this was a lot of information to absorb and process. In the following pages you will find my **MODERN Stress Management (MSM)** brochure, which covers the main principles of MSM in a nutshell.

Our MSM facilitators give talks and a full day's training based on this information, where participants can try out the effects of working with energy in mind first hand. We also provide personalised MODERN Stress Management programs to individuals, families, institutions, teams and companies, and we can train your own people to work with MSM.

If you are interested in developing a unique and personalised MSM program for your company or institution, please contact us. Having stress aware people around will give you an enormous competitive advantage that will translate directly to your bottom line, no matter how you would like to measure this.

Money can't buy happiness - but becoming energy aware and adding that essential 16.7% of information which connects the dots to your reality absolutely can. Happiness on a whole new level, at that.

Just to remind us and answer the question as to why one might want to really focus on the energy levels and actual, real, MODERN stress management, a highlight from the brochure which stood out to me.

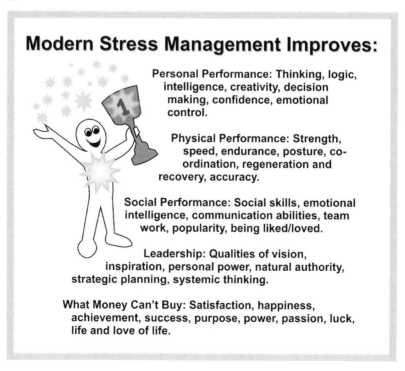

Modern Stress Management Improves:

Personal Performance: Thinking, logic, intelligence, creativity, decision making, confidence, emotional control.

Physical Performance: Strength, speed, endurance, posture, co-ordination, regeneration and recovery, accuracy.

Social Performance: Social skills, emotional intelligence, communication abilities, team work, popularity, being liked/loved.

Leadership: Qualities of vision, inspiration, personal power, natural authority, strategic planning, systemic thinking.

What Money Can't Buy: Satisfaction, happiness, achievement, success, purpose, power, passion, luck, life and love of life.

There has never been a product that promised all of that before - and actually delivered it.

With MODERN Stress Management, you don't have to change your religion or join a cult. You don't have to subscribe to a program that will cost you a fortune and lead to nothing much in the end.

An intelligent person, armed with this one little book, has the key to transform their own life and turn stress to success, literally, in their real world days and nights, in their real world reality.

Any such person becomes a seed of change, because as they change their energy states and behaviours, they influence everyone around them.

This is a cumulative change and I have high hopes for this.

In essence, becoming energy aware and transmitting the 16.7% additional information requires nothing more than that a person should have understood it themselves, and the rest you can draw with a stick in the sand.

I decided at the very young age that I would try and change the world.

After an entire lifetime spent on the project, this is how I'm going to do it.

By offering those who would want it that seemingly small but absolutely essential 16.7% of information, unlocked.

If you can't see, but actually SENSE the sense in this, I welcome you to MSM.

Let's do it.

Let's change the world!

Welcome To Modern Stress Management!

We are excited and delighted to introduce you to a new and different way to understand, measure and transcend stress in your life, and that of other people.

The information and practices you will be learning are easy, natural and make perfect sense.

You can rest assured that these new approaches to stress management have been tried and tested for three decades and with millions of real people from all around the world.

In the process of this, it has become possible for men, women and children to take a fresh, new approach to stress which makes it simple and humane to reverse stress - to quite literally, turn from stress towards success.

From Stress To Success

Amongst the many problems with the old stress management approaches was that they stopped too soon - the goal was "to find peace," or "just not to be so stressed all the time any longer."

It turns out that this isn't a goal, and in fact makes any kind of stress mangement difficult, if not entirely impossible.

"Stress" is a code word for negative emotions - being nervous, being anxious, being afraid, getting angry, losing control over our emotions. People have tried to be more "emotionless" - but that's not the answer.

In order to truly overcome stress, we need to engage the power of positive emotions.

By setting the goal towards positive emotions, we move naturally into the realms of the high energy states - empowering emotions, in other words. We are naturally designed to move towards happiness, and away from fear and terror. When we work with our natural systems, we gain emotional control, and the ability to get out of stress fast.

The world we live in is stressful. Yet we can learn to work with our emotions and our energy system in the right way. When we do, we start to "feel better" - immediately. We also naturally start to "think better" and our bodies become faster, stronger and healthier.

The benefits from managing your stress and those of the people around you in a new and better way are astonishing.

Allow yourself to be amazed and excited what MODERN Stress Management can do for you.

Best of all, now "peace and quiet" is no longer the goal, but instead high energy states that are empowering, delightful, feel good and make us much, much happier.

That's a wonderful thing and we're glad that you are here!

Enjoy "MODERN Stress Management" - and let's make the world a better place, one less stressed, happier human being at a time!

With best wishes,

Silvia Hartmann

Chair, The Guild of Energists GOE
www.GOE.ac

What Causes Stress?

Everybody knows that you are more stressed when ...

- Hungry
- Thirsty
- Tired
- Hung Over
- In Pain, Sick or Ill

That's not the whole story though.

There is something important missing from our understanding of stress.

What could it possibly be ...?

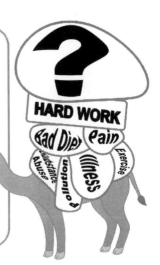

The big X-Factor is:

Emotional Stress.

**Emotions are
physical feelings in the body
that have no physical origin.**

"You know those feelings, when your hands go cold, your stomach starts to churn, your head feels hot, your neck feels tight, your legs go weak?

"That's what other people call emotions!"

Dealing with Emotional Stress
is what MODERN Stress Management offers.

We understand that stress is not "in the head," it's in the body instead.

That is why stressed people get sick - in exactly the same place where they "carry their stress in their body."

"Where do you feel your stress in your body?
"Show me with your hands!"

Meet Your Energy Body!

People have a physical body.

They also have an energy body.

The energy body transmit how it is doing through "emotions" - physical sensations that have no physical origin.

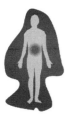

We can't see the energy body.

We sense it through our 6th Sense.

The 6th Sense sensations include:
- Intution/Gut Response
- Emotions
- Psychosomatic Pain

- People today are much more stressed than they think they are.
- Negative energy states are the norm. They are even encouraged because stressed people tend to run around more and seem to be more active.
- No stress is good for you.
- All stress creates disturbances and makes people more stupid, more clumsy, and less able to make good decisions.
- "Optimal performance" is found ONLY on the Positive Side of the Stress Chart, nowhere else.
- The really high energy states were previously thought to be attainable only by prophets, saints and Zen Masters - this is incorrect.
- Every normal human being has their own +10.
- To reach +10, we need to make ourselves and others HAPPIER.
- This can't be done by eating stuff or buying stuff, it's a matter of energy.
- Any movement UP the energy chart takes you out of stress, and towards success.

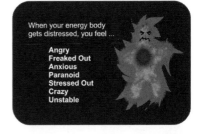

When your energy body is constantly low on energy, you feel ...

Sad
"Blue"
Powerless
Miserable
Helpless
Alone
Unlovable

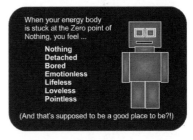

When your energy body gets distressed, you feel ...

Angry
Freaked Out
Anxious
Paranoid
Stressed Out
Crazy
Unstable

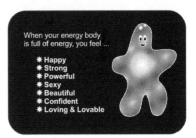

When your energy body is stuck at the Zero point of Nothing, you feel ...

Nothing
Detached
Bored
Emotionless
Lifeless
Loveless
Pointless

(And that's supposed to be a good place to be?!)

When your energy body is full of energy, you feel ...

✻ Happy
✻ Strong
✻ Powerful
✻ Sexy
✻ Beautiful
✻ Confident
✻ Loving & Lovable

When your energy body hits +10, THAT is "**the real you**" and you are ...

✻ Amazing
✻ Attractive
✻ Powerful
✻ Intelligent
✻ Creative
✻ Inspiring
✻ Magical

You are the best YOU you can possibly be!

The Energy Body Stress Chart

-10	So much stress damage that the system does not restore itself (catatonia)
- 9	Very, very high stress triggers a shut down of the totality (panic attack followed by unconsciousness)
- 8	Very high stress causes extremely severe disturbances (self mutilation, blind rage, "going berserk," "madness")
- 7	Very high stress causing extreme disturbances (extreme temper tantrums, self abuse, schizophrenic metaphors, "crazy ideas")
- 6	High stress causing high disturbances (temper tantrums, high end addictions, illogical thinking, immediate gratification, unstable, highly egocentric)
- 5	Full stress causing the symptoms normally associated with stress (irritability, inability to concentrate, not in control of thoughts and memories, communication failures, inability to enter rapport with another)
- 4	General stress (lapses in ability to control thoughts, emotions and behaviour, lack of long term planning ability, overexcited, overly (...), stubborn, closed mind, impaired communication skills)
- 3	Medium stress (talking, thinking and moving a too fast, trying to do too much, putting in more effort than the situation requires, lack of empathy)
- 2	Low Stress (slight impairment in emotional control, not entirely "clear" on future goals and current situations, slight impairment in social skills)
- 1	Very low stress (occasional flashes of uninvited thoughts and negative internal representations)
	No stress and no energy (calm, tranquil, peaceful, no action required, resting, relaxing)
+1	Very low energy flow (neutral, aware, occasional flashes of positive/interesting internal representations and emotions)
+2	Low energy flow (vague sense of potential, hope, feeling like "waking up from a sleep")
+3	Medium energy flow (sense of wellness, feeling ok, smiling, beginning to move, enjoying the present)
+4	Improving energy flow (breathing deeply, increased body awareness, more movement, feeling good, starting to think about the future, able and willing to communicate freely)
+5	General energy flow (feeling wide awake, happy, ready for action, wanting to take action, wanting to interact and communicate)
+6	Faster energy flow (feeling exciting physical sensations, more expansive thinking, feeling personally powerful, feeling excited, enjoying communication, high social awareness)
+7	Very fast energy flow (re-thinking and re-organising concepts, expanded awareness, feeling powerful positive emotions, feeling alive, feeling love)
+8	High energy flow (picking up personal power, feeling delighted, making new decisions, very fast and very logical thinking, high social abilities of rapport and communication)
+9	Very high energy flow (delighted, unable to sit still, tingling all over, very excited, joyful, actively loving)
+10	Optimal energy flow (enlightenment experience, unconditional love)

EVERY person "improves" in EVERY WAY when we re-energize the energy body.

Are you a stressed -5, or are you an excited +5 ?
Easy! Excited feels good, and stress feels bad.

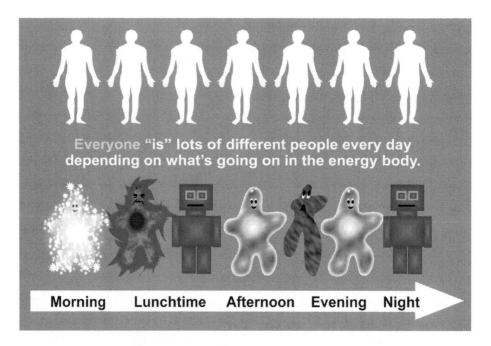

Everyone "is" lots of different people every day depending on what's going on in the energy body.

Morning   Lunchtime   Afternoon   Evening   Night

Modern Stress Management Improves:

Personal Performance: Thinking, logic, intelligence, creativity, decision making, confidence, emotional control.

Physical Performance: Strength, speed, endurance, posture, co-ordination, regeneration and recovery, accuracy.

Social Performance: Social skills, emotional intelligence, communication abilities, team work, popularity, being liked/loved.

Leadership: Qualities of vision, inspiration, personal power, natural authority, strategic planning, systemic thinking.

What Money Can't Buy: Satisfaction, happiness, achievement, success, purpose, power, passion, luck, life and love of life.

160

Modern Stress Management works by:

1. Recognising your stress levels.

2. Taking immediate action to stabilize.

3. Raising energy to get out of stress, and into the positive side of the SUE Scale.

Success lies on the other side of ZERO!

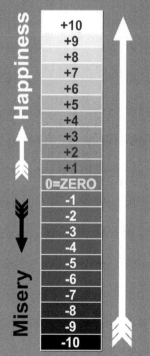

Fill Your Batteries of Life!

Happiness

+10
+9
+8
+7
+6
+5
+4
+3
+2
+1
0=ZERO
-1
-2
-3
-4
-5
-6
-7
-8
-9
-10

Misery

What raises YOUR energy?

161

Easy Energy Raising Techniques
Choose the one you like most.

1. Where are you on the SUE Scale right now?

2. Do the energy technique of your choice:

Heart Power
Place your hands on your energy heart and
breathe in and out deeply.
Very easy to do, this stabilises the energy system
and raises energy fast.

Positive Energy EFT
Simply tap or touch the special energy points
and say the name of something you want more of
in your life, such as power, love, energy or success.
Effective and easy.

Mind Power
Use the "Instant Holiday" experience to give your
energy body a time of relaxing and re-charging
your batteries of life.

3. What is your SUE Number now?

Do it more than once
and get your energy HIGHER!

 # Heart Power

The "Heart of Energy" is the power centre of the energy body.

- Point to your chest with your leading hand to find your heart centre.
- Place the palm of your leading hand on that spot, then place the other hand on top.
- This is The Heart Position.
- Notice the sensations of your hands on your chest.
- Take three deep slow breaths, in and out.

Three easy Heart Power Exercises:

Something To Love	Breathe Out Stress, Breathe In Success	Here & Now
In the Heart Position, keep breathing and think of some one or somet hing you .really love. Focus on how it makes you feel inside.	In the Heart Position, breathe out your stress on the out breath, and on the in breath, breathe in fresh air and energy.	In the Heart Position, breathe deeply. Note what you can see, hear, feel, scent, taste and how you feel inside (6th Sense).

Disturbed System/Stress ➤➤——➤										Nothing	➤➤		——➤				Powerful/Healthy System		
-10	-9	-8	-7	-6	-5	-4	-3	-2	-1	0	+1	+2	+3	+4	+5	+6	+7	+8	+9	+10
Negative Emotions ➤➤——➤										NO Emotions	➤➤		——➤				Positive Emotions		

Use the Heart Position at any time to stabilise yourself, to stop stress from escalating, and to raise energy.

Good Energy With Positive EFT

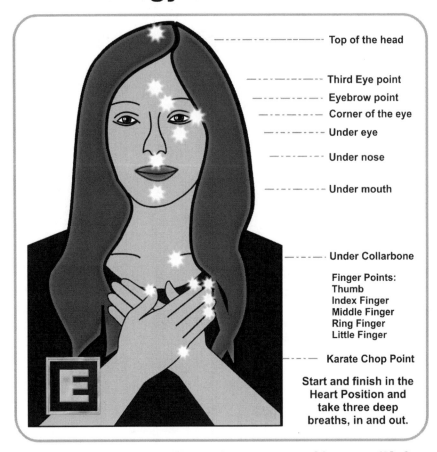

- Top of the head
- Third Eye point
- Eyebrow point
- Corner of the eye
- Under eye
- Under nose
- Under mouth
- Under Collarbone

Finger Points:
Thumb
Index Finger
Middle Finger
Ring Finger
Little Finger

- Karate Chop Point

Start and finish in the
Heart Position and
take three deep
breaths, in and out.

**What would you like to have more of in your life?
Tap or simply touch all the points and say the word.**

For a real
energy
boost, do all
9 - which
one do you
pick first ...?

Energy	Happiness	Success
Power	Love	Money
Vitality	Clarity	Confidence

164

Take A Mini Holiday!

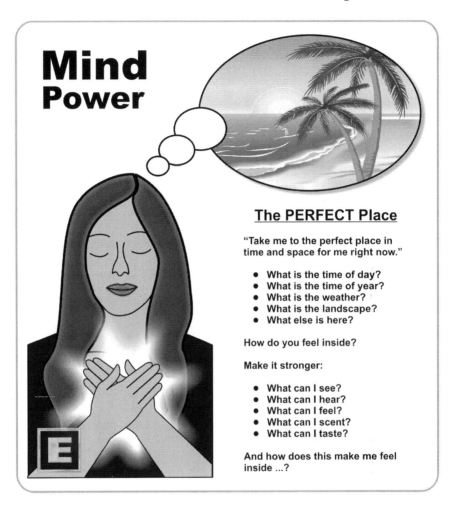

Mind Power

The PERFECT Place

"Take me to the perfect place in time and space for me right now."

- What is the time of day?
- What is the time of year?
- What is the weather?
- What is the landscape?
- What else is here?

How do you feel inside?

Make it stronger:

- What can I see?
- What can I hear?
- What can I feel?
- What can I scent?
- What can I taste?

And how does this make me feel inside ...?

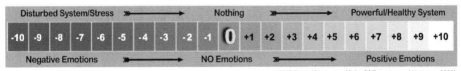

Disturbed System/Stress ➤➤➤➤									Nothing		➤➤➤				Powerful/Healthy System		
-10	-9	-8	-7	-6	-5	-4	-3	-2	-1	0	+1	+2	+3	+4	+5	+6	+7	+8	+9	+10
Negative Emotions ➤➤➤							NO Emotions		➤➤➤			Positive Emotions		

SUE Scale (Subjective Units Of Experience, Hartmann 2009)

Always check with the SUE Scale where you are.

Raise more energy to get even higher!

Achieve Goals & Set NEW Goals!

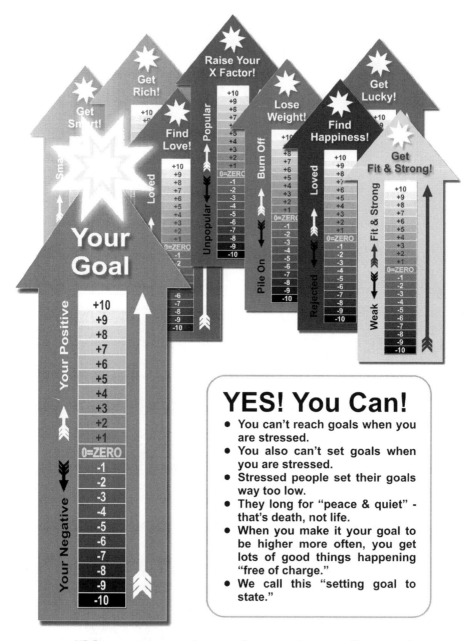

YES! You Can!

- You can't reach goals when you are stressed.
- You also can't set goals when you are stressed.
- Stressed people set their goals way too low.
- They long for "peace & quiet" - that's death, not life.
- When you make it your goal to be higher more often, you get lots of good things happening "free of charge."
- We call this "setting goal to state."

"You can set goals and reach goals when you are energized."

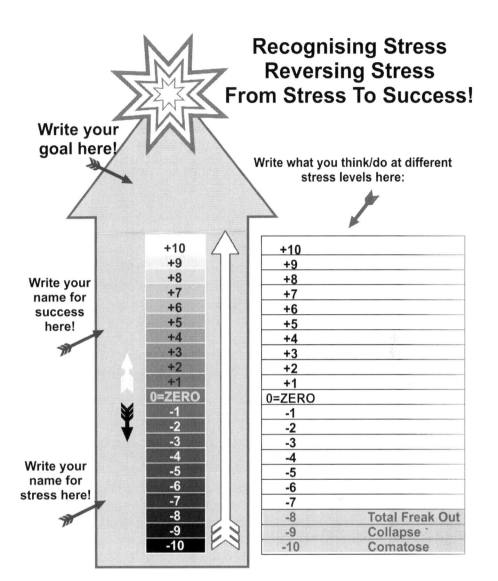

Recognising Stress
Reversing Stress
From Stress To Success!

Write your goal here!

Write what you think/do at different stress levels here:

Write your name for success here!

Write your name for stress here!

+10		
+9		
+8		
+7		
+6		
+5		
+4		
+3		
+2		
+1		
0=ZERO		
-1		
-2		
-3		
-4		
-5		
-6		
-7		
-8	Total Freak Out	
-9	Collapse	
-10	Comatose	

1. LEARN what you think, say to yourself, say to others, what you do and how you feel at the different stress/energy levels.
2. USE this so you KNOW when you are getting too low on energy.
3. ENERGIZE as soon as possible for your best performance!

Is All Your Stress Really "Your" Stress?

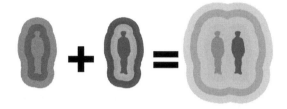 The Couple Bubble

 The Couple Bubble
(with another social mammal)

 The Group Bubble

- People are naturally designed to form energetic relationships.
- Their energy systems connect up and they form "couple bubbles" and "group bubbles."
- People also bubble with companion animals.
- The bubble (the partnership, the team, the family etc.) is more than the sum of its parts and an entity in its own right.
- Stress can infect others in a bubble.
- The higher the energy of all participants in a bubble, the better it feels and the more it uplifts each individual in the bubble.

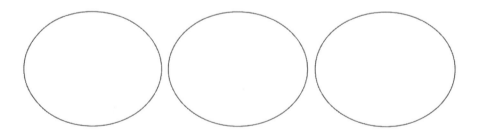

What are your main bubbles?

The YES Principle

Going UP:
YES!

Going DOWN:
NO!

Going UP: YES!	Going DOWN: NO!
Yes	No
Future	Past
Right	Wrong
Good	Bad
Attention	Ignorance
Solution	Problem
Positive	Negative
Connection	Isolation
Acceptance	Judgement
Agree	Disagree
Praise	Criticism
Love	Hate

- Raising energy in any bubble is the first order of business.
- We can't begin to solve problems unless we are on the positive side.
- Once we are higher, we can solve problems from the higher/better state.

The higher the energy in any bubble,
the more transformational the solutions.

The higher <u>you</u> are, the easier it is
to raise other people's energy.

Raise <u>YOUR</u> energy FIRST!
<u>YOUR</u> happiness <u>MATTERS</u>!

MODERN Leadership

Spheres of
Influence

+5
+6
+7
+8
+9
+10

- **The person with the best energy system is naturally the leader of the group.**
- **The higher on the SUE Scale you are, the "bigger" your energy system becomes.**
- **The higher you are, the greater your sphere of influence becomes.**

Empowering yourself makes you a <u>natural</u> leader.

Empowering People

The old "Hitler Model"
One "giant leader" standing on top
of a highly stressed population
who can't think for themselves.

The "King Arthur" Model
This may start with one visionary leader but the leader
makes it their business to empower everyone else so that
a super-powerful "group bubble" comes into being.

MODERN Leadership is about raising everyone's
energy so that each individual becomes the
best person they can be.

Together, highly energized people
have the power to change the world - <u>FAST.</u>

Your Happiness Matters!

⭐ Love	⭐ Strength	⭐ Time
⭐ Youth	⭐ Genius	⭐ Harmony
⭐ Family	⭐ Mystery	⭐ Intelligence
⭐ Laughter	⭐ Brilliance	⭐ Vision
⭐ Wisdom	⭐ Sunshine	⭐ Abundance
⭐ Wealth	⭐ Money	⭐ Beauty
⭐ Luck	⭐ Energy	⭐ Health
⭐ Respect	⭐ Happiness	⭐ Control
⭐ Logic	⭐ Certainty	⭐ Space
⭐ Play	⭐ Wisdom	⭐ Success
⭐ Creativity	⭐ Serenity	⭐ Purpose
⭐ Sensuality	⭐ Inspiration	⭐ Gold
⭐ Wonder	⭐ Freedom	⭐ Energy
⭐ Power	⭐ Romance	⭐ Clarity
⭐ Confidence	⭐ Joy	⭐ Vitality

- Positive Energy is FREE.
- Use it to empower your energy body, to get out of stress and give you the energy for achiving YOUR success in the real world.
- What do you want more of in your life?
- You can have anything as an energy - rock star energy, Superman energy, diamond energy, Lamborghini energy, red carpet energy, Einstein energy - to inspire you.
- Use your own hopes and dreams, needs and wants to guide you to the energy you need to succeed.
- Take as much energy as you want - energy is truly infinite and there's enough for everyone!

The more you have, the more you have to give.

E Is For ENERGY

The Guild of Energists began in 1998 as The Association For Meridian & Energy Therapies The AMT to bring MODERN energy work into the mainstream.

Based on modern, logical research instead of "the Chinese Whispers of the ages," free from religious content, practical and most of all useful, modern energy work acknowledges the reality of the human energy body.

Modern energy work defines emotions as feedback devices for the state of the energy body, and demystifies the 6th sense.

Modern energy work is "The Third Field" which has been missing from science and research. Medical science deals with the body, psychology with the mind. The Third Field of modern energism deals with emotions, and with the energy body.

Silvia Hartmann's breakthrough research into energetic relationships, which began in 1988 and led eventually to the formulation of the SUE Scale (2009), The Energy Body Stress Chart (2011), and The Pyramid Model for Modern Stress Management (2015) has produced a practical, sensible approach from which all people can benefit.

Understanding energy body stress is the first step to finding new solutions in our complex and demanding modern world. Then, moving from stress to success gives us the energy, strength and intelligence to make our lives a better, happier and more empowered place - one person at a time.

Join The Guild of Energists

GOE is an association of people who understand the reality of "energy" - not because they "believe in it" but because they have experienced the effects in their own lives, and know that energy is very real. Our members come from all walks of life, all religious backgrounds, from all around the world. We have one thing in common:

We ♥ Energy!

Join The Guild of Energists - and receive "The Energist," the world's first magazine dedicated to all things energy. Filled with case stories, tips and news from around the world, you become part of a vibrant international community at the very leading edge of modern energism.

www.GOE.ac

Further Information

Extreme Stress/Chronic Stress

People's energy bodies have been completely ignored, and some people's energy bodies are in much worse shape than others.

The energy body can sustain significant injuries due to "trauma" - in fact, trauma is what an energy body injury actually is.

Many, many more people than you would have ever guessed suffer from extreme stress and chronic stress (being constantly stuck at -5 or even below, with very little upward movement, if any at all) because of injuries to the energy body.

"Talking about it" doesn't heal energy body injuries.

You actually get much better results with simple "laying on of hands" than you do with talking about how much it hurts and why, and who did what to whom, over and over again.

We now have a thing called "Energy Psychology" which is a blending of talking about it and doing energy treatments at the same time. This is massively more effective when it comes to treating energy body injuries, but in my opinion, still only a step stone to the proper and direct treatment of the energy body.

If you are suffering from extreme stress or chronic stress, I strongly recommend to get in touch with a modern energist as soon as possible.

Unlike the old psycho- approaches, you do not have to re-live a single thing nor do you need to "talk about it" - unless you really want to.

Modern energy work - which includes the healing and nourishment of the neglected energy body - is powerful, direct, and a positive experience of real healing. The pain goes away, the burdens are released and the person can breathe again.

You will find many wonderful modern energists to get you started on your healing journey in our world wide register at www.goe.ac

I strongly recommend if you are chronically or severely stressed to work with a practitioner to get you started right. You can't do your own heart and lung transplant, and likewise, if you have suffered from severe energy body injuries, you need help NOW.

Find a modern energy healing practitioner at

www.GOE.ac
The Guild of Energists

Learn More Advanced Modern Energy Techniques

There were three basic modern energy raising techniques outlined at the end of the book - 1. Heart Power, 2. Positive EFT and 3. Mind Power. Different people prefer different approaches, so here is how to learn more about your favourite de-stressing/re-energizing method.

1. Heart Power - This comes from the EMO Energy In Motion system which is new to the 21st Century and embodies how modern energists work with the energy body - directly through the 6th Sense. EMO greatly increases your ability to handle all forms of energies, significantly improves flow of energy through the energy body, and is the favourite technique for people who love energy and can't wait to unlock more of the amazing potential of modern energy work on every level.

Start with Silvia's book on EMO - Oceans of Energy, The Patterns & Techniques of EMO Energy In Motion.

You can find more in-depth and professional courses in EMO at www.GOE.ac

2. Positive EFT - This comes from modern Energy EFT, a descendant of the original Classic EFT (Emotional Freedom Techniques). Energy EFT is extremely flexible, easy to use and brings great results, even with absolute energy newbies.

Start with Silvia's book Positive EFT. If you want to learn more, there is Energy EFT, which can also be used as a reference for professional energists as it contains a comprehensive A-Z of treatment methods and scripts for a wide variety of emotional problems.

You can find a variety of different courses on modern Energy EFT as well as helpful practitioners at www.GOE.ac

3. Mind Power - The "Instant Holiday" is an example of the Classic Game from the original Project Sanctuary program by Silvia Hartmann. To learn more about this area of modern energism, which deals with the energy mind, genius, metaphor, paranormal language, autogenics and imagination, start with "Infinite Creativity" by Silvia Hartmann.

Learn More About Events Psychology

We recommend to start with "Events Psychology - How to understand yourself and other people." This book contains also information on The Guiding Stars - highly charged positive events that underlie the formation of addictions, fetishes and philias, as well as other types of energy body events, including missing events, and how to work with memories in a far more elegant and successful fashion. The SUE Scale and the Aspects Model are outlined here too. Essential reading for modern energists and all those who want answers that current psychology doesn't provide.

175

Join The Guild of Energists

The Guild of Energists is the only organisation in the world that deals with reasonable, rational, provable modern energism. We have personal membership for individuals who love energy for self help and personal advancement; there is professional membership for modern energists who work as coaches, counsellors, therapists and healers; and there is the trainer's membership for those who teach and train others in modern energy work.

Our members come from all walks of life, we are all real people together on an amazing journey of personal discovery and empowerment. We share insights and experiences through our online forums, newsletters, our print magazine, The Energist, and our conferences.

We welcome clear thinking, success orientated people to come and join us and help us make the world a happier place. Then the world can't but help become a better place as well!

Links In Brief

- About Modern Energism: Visit The Guild of Energists: **GOE.ac**
- Find a Modern Stress Management Facilitator to work with you, your company or your team: **GOE.ac**
-

Non Fiction Books By Silvia Hartmann

- Zauberwelt: A simple first introduction to the worlds of modern energy work.
- EMO - Energy In Motion: Learn about your energy body, energy nutrition, energy body health & fitness and how to master your emotions.
- Positive EFT: Learn a useful life skill to raise energy fast and reliably for yourself, with partners and in groups.
- Energy EFT: Advanced EFT information for professional counsellors and therapists.
- Infinite Creativity: Silvia Hartmann's autobiography.
- Events Psychology: How to understand yourself, and other people.

DragonRising.com

"If this book has been exceedingly valuable to you, or to someone you love; if what you have learned here has significantly helped you, your family or your company; if it has saved and/or made you exponentially more money, please consider a "Thank You!" donation." GOE.ac

About The Author

Silvia Hartmann was born in Germany in 1959 and moved to the United Kingdom in 1978. She began working with applied animal behaviour and developed *The Harmony Program*, the result of an investigation into Rage Syndrome and outlining the Attention Seeking Behaviour Scale for the first time in 1993.

Switching to human behaviour, Silvia Hartmann studied hypnosis, NLP and General Semantics, specialising in the decoding of metaphor. Her seminal work on immersive communication with the unconscious mind, *Project Sanctuary*, was published in 1996.

In 1998, she came across EFT Emotional Freedom Techniques and decided to investigate this further. Her book, *Adventures in EFT*, went through 8 Editions and was for the first three years the only book published on EFT at that time. She also wrote the first modern energy work based training course for the Association For Meridian & Energy Therapies in 1999 which was taught around the world unchanged until 2011.

In 2002, she switched from EFT to *EMO Energy In Motion* as a primary research tool for modern energy work. She formulated the Energy Body Stress Chart, the SUE Scale, described the processes of Guiding Star formation and developed the Aspects Model from 2002 to 2009, culminating in the publication of the groundbreaking *Events Psychology*.

In 2011, Silvia Hartmann created a new training program for EFT practitioners worldwide, based on the advanced energy information from EMO and Events Psychology, including *Positive EFT* which is designed to teach users about "the white space of positive emotions" which had been missing from the original trainings materials.

In 2012, she demonstrated the power of using energy raising techniques to produce reliable and consistently high quality creative outcomes by writing a fiction novel live online in front of a world wide audience using Google Docs. *The Dragon Lords* is now listed in "The History of The Book In 100 Books" (British Library Publication) and was launched at Google's headquarters in London, England.

During an energy art project in 2012, Silvia Hartmann became aware of "The Trillion Dollar Stress Pandemic" and decided to do something about it. She spent the following year on the road, driving through England, Ireland, and the USA to learn more about what real people think and feel.

MODERN Stress Management was the outcome of this long term project, and a renewed determination to let people know about the reality of energy, to put them in a position to make up their own minds at last. *The Trillion Dollar Stress Solution*, 1st Edition, was published in 2015.

Silvia Hartmann's work has been translated into over 50 languages, and her books have been published in the United Kingdom, the United States, Canada, Australia, Germany, Spain, the Czech republic, Italy and Brazil. She is currently the trainings director and chair of The Guild of Energists, a world wide membership organisation dedicated to bringing love and logic to the modern world.

Silvia Hartmann does not have a Wikipedia page.